THE NATURAL HOME

THE NATURAL HOME

Photography: Tim Clinch, Tim Beddow, Simon McBride und Francesco Venturi

Printed and bound by: Neue Stalling, Oldenburg

Printed and bound in Germany ISBN 3-7701-7009-1

Content

Mediterranean Lifestyle

Perfect Restoration

The well-known Milan-based interior designer Piero Castellini was looking for a country home large enough to provide a comfortable retreat for his entire family to enjoy on holiday.

The farmhouse he found in the Tuscan hills just south of Siena fitted the bill. When he first discovered Le Fontanelle he immediately saw the potential of the dilapidated farmhouse. His first

LEFT Blue-green shutters and doors punctuate the golden hues of the exterior stucco, while climbing roses soften the austere lines of the house. Further devices to beautify the otherwise plain facade include hand-thrown terracotta urns planted with geraniums.

OPPOSITE A pair of riding boots sits waiting at the entrance to the house. The Louis XVI sofa is covered in a Pierre Frey fabric.

decision was to strip the house down to its bare fabric, revealing ancient stone, beams and brick. Yet this was not to be a typical restoration, with emphasis on rustic and humble origins. Instead, Castellini took as his starting point the strong voice of the surrounding countryside, intent on capturing the same rugged texture and intensity of the colours visible outside.

The decoration of the house very much reflects the designer's own taste and pays homage to his personal brand of sophisticated eclecticism. No rough farm tables here. In their place, exquisite examples from various periods intermingle: Louis XVI, Chinese colonial, and neoclassical statuary all have their place.

The most unique aspect of the house is its use of colour. For help in capturing the look and feel of the Tuscan palette, he turned to artist Adam Alvarez, a Briton transplanted to Chianti. Using only natural pigments, he created almost transparent layers of colour that suffuse the rooms as the light pours through the windows. The ground floor is dominated by warm tones of

1800

OPPOSITE & RIGHT Much of daily life at the house revolves around Piero Castellini's stable of horses. Saddles stand ready outside the stables for a mid-morning ride. In the kitchen, an iron crockery stand displays a collection of antique plates.

ochre and yellow, while the upper floor gives way to a cooler range of violets and blues.

Bathrooms as well are given the full Castellini treatment. Rather than making each different, he chose the pleasing palette of ivory and terracotta, played out in differing patterns, for each of the rooms. Alvarez applied his magic on the walls, while the floors were laid out in a checker-board pattern of unwaxed matt tiles.

Castellini is known for his attention to detail, and every object in his own house reflects this approach. The quality of the bed-linen or the types of herbs in the garden are as important to him as the beams that support the roof or the size of the windows that break the facade. All work together harmoniously. A recur-

RIGHT In stark contrast to the dark cellars below ground, the living areas of the Castellini house are awash with zinging colours. The corridor that runs the length of the upper floor is painted in warm yellows. All the rooms lead off the corridor, including the violet-blue study just visible.

RIGHT An adjoining kitchen and dining area provide a focus for meal times. The warm yellow walls, terracotta floors and abundance of natural light make this one of the most inviting parts of the house. The dining room is given over to a large cherrywood table and a selection of eighteenth- and nineteenth-century lacquered chairs. Local cheeses, salami, prosciutto and bread provide an impromptu lunch, accompanied by red wine bought from the cantina next door and decanted into a carafe.

OPPOSITE, ABOVE & RIGHT The study adjoins the master bedroom and provides a space for Castellini to read and work on his architectural projects. A hand-tinted paint washes the room in a calming sea of blue, echoed in the ticking covering the day bed. The mantelpiece supports a collection of blue porcelain; an eighteenth-century Piedmontese cameo hangs above. Original terracotta flooring and exposed beams lend the room a warm rustic quality.

ring theme throughout the house is Castellini's passion for beautiful fabrics. Indian cotton saris float from a four poster bed in one room, while formal toile-de-Jouys are used in another. Although textures and prints change from room to room, they are united by the designer's personal vision.

LEFT & ABOVE The soaring arches that frame the main living room are an original part of this suite of ground-floor rooms. Shades of orange and ochre encase the spacious room, the seemingly perfect colour composition broken only by the blackened surround of the fireplace. Above the mantelpiece, a collection of miniature eighteenth-century plaster portraits is enclosed in a frame.

Current Vintage

LEFT & ABOVE The sober lines of Tenuta di Trinoro are reflected in a shallow manmade pond. Empty wine casks are stacked in the shade, waiting to be cleaned and refilled with the fruit of the year's harvest.

LEFT The collection of buildings includes a medieval tower, its entrance marked by a vivid cupola. The brightly coloured folly was added by the owner, Andrea Franchetti, and pays homage to the days of the Crusades, when the original watchtower was always manned.

It is appropriate that Tenuta di Trinoro is the name of both the robust red wine that Italian vintner Andrea Franchetti produces and the Tuscan home overlooking his vineyards.

One led to the other and they are part of the complicated story that brought him, and keeps him, in southern Tuscany. Franchetti knew the area well, having visited the homes of friends and family since he was a child. In 1981 he finally bought himself a cluster of old farmhouses, all sadly neglected and half collapsed. Restoring first one and then another, he found himself slipping slowly into the country way of life, further and further away from his career as a wine distributor in New York.

How to remain in the area, supporting his passion for restoring old houses, as well as continuing to use his experience in the field of wine? In 1990 he planted the first vines on his property, intent on producing a big, full-bodied red wine. The fruits of his labour were harvested in 1995 and are now on the market under his label 'Tenuta di Trinoro'. While the area has no great wine-growing tradition comparable to that of nearby Montalcino, all Italian appellations are a relatively new development and Franchetti is just one of a growing number of enthusiasts intent on producing new and important wines.

Franchetti's home, which is really a collection of several buildings, overlooks the Val d'Orcia, a magical valley that lies along the southern border of Tuscany. Views from the upper windows take in the vast sweep of northern Tuscany. The days of border

OPPOSITE The ground floor, as in all Tuscan country homes, was originally used as an animal stall. Sunlight illuminates what now serves as a spacious kitchen.

OPPOSITE & ABOVE Details of life at Tenuta di Trinoro: the cellar entrance and staples of robust Tuscan cooking.

controls are long past, but the medieval tower which forms the nucleus of one of the houses is testament to the precarious position of these outposts. Perched atop the ridge, a series of such towers could pass messages from one to the next, all the way back to Florence.

Franchetti's life is divided between his houses. Sleeping in one, he may decide to breakfast in another and then go back to the first for a mid-afternoon siesta. The interiors reflect this casual outlook and are a mixture of textures and colours that reflect his personal taste.

As far as possible during the restoration, materials were left as they were found. The top level of one of the buildings was in such good shape that the entire original floor, constructed out of handmade terracotta tiles, was retained, receiving only a clean-up and a coat of wax. While most of the roofing had to be patched, aged local tiles were used to retain the original effect. One exception is the hot pink cupola which tops a doorway. This was Franchetti's addition and its Eastern feeling pays poetic homage to the days of the Crusades, when the watchtower was always manned.

The ogive arches over some of the doors are original thirteenth-century architectural elements.

LEFT Vineyards march across the valley. Cabernet Franc, Cabernet Sauvignon and Merlot varieties are blended with Petit Verdot and a mixture of Italian grapesto to produce Franchetti's wine.

Newer additions are the stretches of exterior paving constructed from river stones. While not a typical Tuscan element, the technique does date back to the Middle Ages, and is often found in fortifications throughout Europe. Although Franchetti chose this pavement for its beauty, it is extremely durable as well, since the stones are sunk to three quarters of their depth into the earth. They will stay in place for decades to come, providing a sound surface over which barrels of wine will clatter on their way to the cellars.

OPPOSITE The furnishing in Franchetti's house is kept to a minimum. Many of the pieces were bought locally and stripped back to reveal their original patinas.

OPPOSITE & LEFT The secluded swimming pool appears to have been carved out of the sheer cliff face. To harmonize with the leafy setting and sea beyond, the pool was lined with a coat of grey emulsion, which gives the water its rich turquoise appearance. Matching turquoise sun loungers complete this idyllic scene.

Ivory Tower

The owners of this villa were looking for the best of all possible worlds when they began their search for a bolt-hole that would offer an alternative to their base in Tuscany. They wanted peace and quiet, an inspiring setting, proximity to both a lively social scene and places of cultural interest, and easy access to the aquatic pursuits for which the Amalfi Coast is justly famous. Their brief was satisfied by an unspoilt corner on Capri.

Sagra
BASSA'
ACIDITA'
OLIO
EXTRA VERGINE
DI OLIVA

PREVIOUS SPREAD & LEFT The steep site is arranged over several terraced levels, each with its own pergola or outdoor furniture. On the main terrace, a rustic reed-covered trellis provides shade during the long hot summer days. Lunch is served at a big wooden farmhouse table surrounded by wicker chairs.

The couple fell in love with Capri's informal yet chic atmosphere and, not surprisingly, its position and brilliant views. They were beguiled not only by its physical beauty, but also by its proximity to the fascinations of the mainland, just a boat ride away. For jet-set village life or even city lights, they could take the ferry to Amalfi. And for intellectual stimulation, they could visit nearby Pompeii to delight in the painted decoration of the villas there, which reveal ancient Roman civilization at its most sophisticated.

As a base for their excursions and adventures, the couple settled on a small house, just big enough to accommodate them comfortably but not so big as to demand time-consuming upkeep. They bought the house from a writer who had constructed it in 1964 as his retreat, and it matched their needs so perfectly that they have changed very little about it. Nevertheless they have made the picturesque villa very much their

own, decorating it with an artful eye that mixes classical antiques with ethnic rugs, textiles and simple earthy furnishings, all set against bright whitewashed walls. Vivid splashes of red, calming sage green, radiant blue and sunny yellow bring a sense of warmth and emotional well-being to the relaxed interiors. The overall mood is one of tranquillity and peace, the perfect place for reviving flagging spirits.

The focal point of this island hideaway is the terrace, divided into several separate living areas: a sweet vine-covered balcony for breakfast caffè latte; a dining alcove furnished with a scrubbed wooden table and wicker chairs; a

OPPOSITE & LEFT In the dining room, a pedestal table is paired with Italian Empire chairs and a white chaise longue studded with gem-like cushions. A bare whitewashed backdrop—typical of houses on Capri—is enlivened with bold splashes of vivid colour, richly decorated textiles and objects collected on the couple's frequent trips abroad. A section of cliff, from which the house was hewn, provides a feature wall in the bedroom, its rough surface offset by piles of luxurious tasselled pillows.

RIGHT In the livingroom, low-level seating, ethnic rugs, stacked baskets and piles of books create a more relaxed mood.

secluded swimming pool; and a sweeping stretch of terracotta-paved patio, set with outdoor sofa and sunloungers. All this overlooks a stunning coastal panorama taking in the port and township of Capri, a vast unbroken swathe of Mediterranean blue and, as the focal point, the Faraglioni—two enormous vol-

canic rocks jutting out of the sea that are symbolic of Capri itself. Whether sitting on the terrace in summer or whiling away the hours in the drawing room during winter, the owners of this villa never cease to delight in the view of the Faraglioni—an ever-present reminder of what drew them here in the first place.

OPPOSITE & RIGHT Most of the summer months are spent on the terrace, relaxing in a generous hammock, eating lunch al fresco or swimming in the saltwater pool. The magnificent views across to Positano are a constant distraction.

Romantic Paradise

On a tiny group of private islands off the coast of Positano sits one of the most unusual homes on the Riviera. It is special not only for its splendid physical setting on one of three jagged rocks rising from the sea, but also for its history. The story of Li Galli, as this tiny archipelago is called, dates back to mythical times, when the Greeks nicknamed it the home of the sirens. Despite the reputation of these beguiling creatures who would lure sailors to their deaths, the dramatic islands of Li Galli have proved compelling to centuries of intrepid seafarers.

In the days of the Emperor Tiberius, a Roman villa was built on Li Galli, perhaps for the emperor himself, who is reputed to have sailed there with his court in the hopes of hearing the sirens singing. Traces of this early habitation of the islands remain, as does a medieval tower built by the Saracens in the eleventh century. They, like others since, prized Li Galli for its strategic significance. However,

LEFT & OPPOSITE The terrace with a fountain was built by Léonide Massine when he lived at Li Galli. The choreographer used the terrace as a stage for dance practice and private performances, but it now serves as the setting for more conventional entertaining. A pair of ornate stone chairs, copies of ancient Roman designs, provide suitably theatrical seating for contemplating the horizon.

it is the most recent residents on the island who have stamped it with their own character to bring this ancient site to life.

The Russian-born choreographer Léonide Massine was responsible for changing the essential nature of the Li Galli archipelago from a place of defence and fortification to a private hideaway. Massine bought the islands in the 1920s, when they had ceased to be of use to anyone strategically, and eventually set about constructing a villa on the site of the original Roman structure. To design the house, he commissioned his friend Le Corbusier, who made the most of the expansive views in his plan. Le Corbusier situated a large terrace garden on the first floor facing Capri and Cape Licosa, and located the bedrooms on the other side of the villa, facing Positano and the Lattari Mountains.

Once the villa was completed, Li Galli became a creative base for Massine. He restored the old watchtower to use as a dance studio and alternative residence, installing a large dance floor, a

ABOVE & RIGHT Present owner Giovanni Russo lives in a Saracen watchtower that dates from the eleventh century, while the two houses on the island provide private quarters for visiting friends.

OPPOSITE & ABOVE The bedrooms in the island's main villa are largely still as Nureyev left them, although much of the furniture was sold at auction. Despite living here for only a few years, Nureyev left an indelible mark on the villa with his vision for a Moorish-style retreat where dancers and choreographers could come for inspiration.

mezzanine that could hold a quartet, and an open-air theatre, since destroyed in a storm. Even after his death in 1979, Massine's passion for dance continued to be played out on the islands when they became a retreat for Rudolf Nureyev. The ballet dancer indulged his passion for the Islamic world, redecorating the villa in the Moorish style and cladding its interiors with specially commissioned tiles. However, the islands served as Nureyev's exotic citadel for just a few years until his death.

By the time Li Galli was bought by its new and current owner, hotelier Giovanni Russo, much had fallen into disrepair. Now restoring it back to life has become Russo's passion. When he is not managing his two hotels in Sorrento, he spends time at Li Galli overseeing work on the buildings and grounds. Summers are spent enjoying the beauty of the islands' unmatched setting, with friends always welcome to share a piece of this private paradise.

Breathing Space

OPPOSITE & ABOVE Both the architecture of the villa and its outlook embody the quintessential Capri. With its plain, whitewashed facade, use of columns, arrangement around an inner courtyard and orientation to the sea, Villa San Michele is characteristic of the style made popular when the Romans colonised the island.

High on a cliff in Anacapri stands the Villa San Michele, where Swedish scientist, scholar, author and philanthropist, Axel Munthe, lived and worked. He began to build this exceptional villa in 1896 after falling in love with the spot during a trip to Naples. In his book, *The History of St Michael*, published in 1940, he vividly described his first encounter with the site, reached after a long climb to a rocky plateau: "The whole Gulf of Naples was at our feet, surrounded by Ischia, Procida, Posillipo, decorated by pines, the scintillating white line of Naples, Vesuvius with its pinkish cloud of smoke, the plains of Sorrento protected by Monte Sant'Angelo and the faraway Apennines covered in snow."

Confronted by this astonishing outlook, Munthe needed little convincing that here was the perfect place to build a house: a place for contemplation, for rest and writing. Inspiring the construction of the villa were the ruins of a small chapel on the site. The vaulted ceiling of the chapel had long since collapsed, leaving large vertical blocks of stone rising out of the rubble of collapsed walls. Its ancient spirit was the catalyst

LEFT & OPPOSITE The villa has been kept much as Axel Munthe left it. Manifestations of antiquity are everywhere, whether in the form of a Grecian-style sculpture flanked by marble columns, a sculpted mask encircled by vines or a mosaic floor inlaid with aquatic motifs.

for the house, which was named, like the chapel, after Saint Michael. The villa was built over a space of five years. Although small in size, with only a handful of rooms, it is the surrounding terraces that lend Villa San Michele its essential character. As Munthe himself described it, there were "… the loggias, the terraces and the bowers all around the villa, where one could look at the sun, the sea, and the clouds—the soul needs more room to breathe than the body."

Architecturally the villa incorporates a harmonious mix of local historical styles. Capri was originally colonized by the ancient Romans and much of the island is still dotted with vestiges of ancient Roman architecture. Later, like other dreamy Riviera settings, it experienced the building boom of the late nineteenth century, evolving its own regional version of the belle époque—a style dubbed "Capreses", a term referring to the rustic, white-washed villas, oriented to the sea and the

OPPOSITE & RIGHT No Italian villa overlooking the coast does without a loggia—a remnant of the ancient Greeks' and Romans' intense relationship with the sky, the sun and the sea. This architectural union of interior and exterior space characterizes both private and public buildings. At Villa San Michele, the loggia serves as a gallery showcasing Axel Munthe's vast collection of antique sculpture and artifacts. Busts mounted on columns and pedestals line the long corridor, while architectural fragments, sculptures and antique furniture jostle for space.

sky, that became the norm in Capri, in stark contrast to the highly ornamental approach associated with the French Riviera. The Villa San Michele incorporates both Roman and Capresian influences, with a beautiful, well-proportioned exterior, arched loggias, vaulted ceilings and classical columns derived from ancient architecture. Mosaic floors, antique sculptures and busts complete the interior scheme. Gardens, terraces and arbours blossom with flowers, paying tribute to the natural flora, as well as the nineteenth-century taste for exotic plants.

It was Axel Munthe's wish that the house he so treasured should become a museum after his death. Fittingly, his former home also plays host to visiting scholars and humanists, who can immerse themselves in the atmosphere that inspired the great visionary, studying not only his philosophies and scientific legacy, but also his finely honed sense of aesthetics.

ABOVE & OPPOSITE A simple and functional kitchen in pristine white is dominated by a monumental tiled unit that serves as work surface, stove top, sink and oven. Original copper pans line the walls and hang from the ceiling. On the terrace, a stone sphinx looks out to sea, a symbol of Munthe's passion for antiquity and archaelogy.

ABOVE The strong architectural lines of the interior are relieved in this drawing room by an injection of soft colour and decorative pattern. Italian furniture, painted in shades of gold and blue, echoes the mosaic floor.

Positano Spirit

When Antonio and Carla Sersale inherited the direction of the renowned Le Sirenuse Hotel in Positano, they lived there for two years while looking for a more intimate base to call home. However, when your family's former country house-cum-hotel is one of the grandest buildings in Positano, boasting a perfect view, everything else seems second best. Eventually though, the couple found just what they wanted: a secluded two-level flat in a 200-year-old UNESCO-listed building, its facade virtually hidden from the hilly street entrance but offering broad glimpses of the sea.

In keeping with the historic significance of their new home, the Sersales created an interior with plenty of authentic local charm. The whitewashed walls and plain tiled floors evoke the natural simplicity of a village house, while providing a backdrop to textiles and furnishings gathered on the couple's travels. Antonio boasts an array of Oriental textiles, carpets, weavings and needlework, bought when he lived for a time

LEFT The bougainvillea-draped terrace is the Sersales' favourite part of the flat. Large glass doors connect it to the lounge and dining rooms, making it an extension of the living areas and allowing sunlight and harbour breezes to filter through.

in Persia. Now the collection includes Indian, Chinese and Turkish pieces as well, which provide striking splashes of colour and texture against the bright white walls. On the terrace, very little in the way of decoration has been required. Here it is the elements of nature that provide the visual interest. Pink bougainvillea drapes itself over the walls, while the photographic coastal views capture the essence of what life in Positano is all about.

ABOVE & OPPOSITE When their busy schedule managing the Sirenuse Hotel allows the couple time off, they indulge their passion for travel to Asia and the Middle East. Exquisite textiles collected en route add luxurious texture and rich colour to the simple white interior spaces with their high ceilings and arched doorways.

LEFT & ABOVE A strong Eastern flavour permeates the interiors, but without compromising their essentially relaxed and rustic atmosphere. A traditional Positano stucco niche melds beautifully with safari chairs, Orientalist textile borders and a Moroccan-style lamp. A terracotta floor and potted palms give the feel of the outdoors.

Pure Country

ABOVE & OPPOSITE Ilaria and Giorgio Miani wanted to preserve the exterior stone wall as far as possible. Where it was crumbling and had to be patched, colour pigments were mixed with the cement to match the weathered look of the rest of the wall. In a protected corner of the garden stand some lounge chairs designed by Ilaria Miani—hidden behind a row of cypresses.

Ilaria and Giorgio Miani are dedicated to the point of obsession to restoring abandoned farmhouses to their original rustic splendour.

It was while touring the winding dirt roads of the Val d'Orcia on their motorbike that the couple came across one of their most charming finds: a ruin of a house overgrown with blackberry thorns and ivy, perched on the edge of a plateau with breathtaking views of the valley below. The Mianis' passion for restoring farmhouses consumes all of their free time—they are always on the lookout for old properties to do up and live in for a while before moving on to the next one—and they knew exactly what they were getting themselves into. This was to be their fourth restoration and they relished the challenge of bringing the old house back to life.

The couple's projects always take their tone from the building itself, regardless of how little is left of it. A bit of coloured plaster still holding on to a crumbling wall, a small carved stone niche, a sagging painted shutter: these are the elements that reveal the soul of the house. In the end, when the work is done, it appears as if the house has always been there, resisting the passage of time yet wearing the years proudly.

The materials used in the construction are all rigorously authentic. The handmade terracotta

RIGHT, ABOVE & OPPOSITE Jars of paint pigment are displayed in a wall niche originally used for storing food, while sheets of Sardinian bread, a handful of dried red chilis and a bottle of olive oil form an impromptu still life. The table and chairs in the kitchen look like originals, but were in fact produced in Ilaria Miani's workshop in Rome.

tiles on the floors are from a neighbouring artisan who still lays them in the sun to bake them to a rich tone. Roof tiles are moss-covered, culled from a nearby ruin. Even the wainscoting, painted by Ilaria Miani herself in bright, saturated colours, reflects local artistic traditions.

The landscape, too, is treated with the same reverence for the past. Obscured by jungle-like vegetation, the original vineyard and olive grove were uncovered and reinstated, and the old crumbling stone walls, used to terrace the sloping terrain, were carefully rebuilt. The original farm-

OPPOSITE & RIGHT The bathroom was originally part of the stairwell. The original steps still cut through one side of the room but now serve as shelves. Shiny tiles are banned from Ilaria Miani's houses—all is kept simple and rustic, including the mirror which is framed with dried flowers.

FOLLOWING SPREAD Grape vines that had been growing on the site for decades were coaxed over a trellis to create a rustic arbour shading an outdoor eating area.

house grounds yielded a vegetable garden and a grape-covered arbour for outdoor meals. The only modern addition was the swimming pool, carefully hidden behind hedges and retaining walls.

It is only in the furnishing that comfort supersedes rusticity. Almost all of the pieces come from Ilaria Miani's atelier in Rome, where she sells exquisitely crafted reproductions of nineteenth-century furnishings. Small side tables, trays and book shelves cosy up to comfortably overstuffed couches and chairs and romantically draped beds.

LEFT & ABOVE The vast bed in the master suite is one of Ilaria Miani's newest creations and incorporates bands of rich colour into a bold design inspired by northern Italian furniture. All the furnishings in the guest room were designed by Ilaria Miani and produced by local craftsmen. The original proportions of the rooms were respected, including the small windows, which frame picture-perfect landscapes.

Pastoral Scenes

In the dramatic countryside outside Montepulciano, a two-tiered loggia provides a formal welcome to the house of Emanuela Stramana and husband Michele Cantatore.

The forms of the sixteenth-century double arches are softened by exuberant Virginia Creeper, which climbs its way up and around the stonework. This imposing facade, however, is somewhat deceptive, as the home that Stramana and Cantatore have created is one of warmth and intimacy, a far cry from the strictures of Renaissance architecture.

Before moving to the country, the couple lived in a formal palace in the centre of Montepulciano. The building had once been home to the Medici family and was carefully restored to its former delicate beauty. But as much as they both loved the palazzo, Stramana and Cantatore felt the need for open spaces and so began the search for a new home. When they found Casteletto, perched high on a hill overlooking local vineyards, fields and farms, the simple villa was in fairly good shape, and they were able to keep renovations to a minimum, re-

LEFT The summer living room is actually a converted carriage house open along one side to catch cooling breezes.

ABOVE Stramana's passion for antique textiles is evident throughout the house. Pieces from her collection appear in nearly every room, even if only a length of lace used to frame a window.

ABOVE The dining room is the most formal area of the house. Even so, the room is far from stuffy. The pristine white walls and lace-trimmed tablecloth are the counterpoint for simple antique furnishings. Bundles of herbs from the kitchen and racks of plates above the sideboard add relaxed touches.

RIGHT The warm tones of antique furnishings mark the living areas and provide the backdrop for refined touches such as the dainty piece of embroidered silk that is pinned to a cupboard door, or the silver tableware that stands on a magnificent bureau. This piece, a studio mobile, *is from central Italy and is more sophisticated in design than most rustic country furniture.*

taining the look and feel of the original structure.

A central courtyard, where animals used to be kept, now provides a focal point for the house. Although the building is quite large—there are seven bedrooms—a feeling of intimacy has been achieved by dividing the house into several smaller, independent suites. Cantatore, an architect who specializes in this type of restoration, converted the ground floor into a large living room and connecting dining room. Antique terracotta tiles pave the floor and an immense fireplace occupies the far end of the room, providing heat for the entire space in the winter months.

The kitchen is Stramana's favourite part of the house. Its generous dimensions remind her of her childhood home, where family life revolved around the kitchen. It provided the setting for all the

OPPOSITE Furnishings in the kitchen are all in the local style, sourced from second-hand shops and antique markets. They are notable for their sturdy, practical nature and comfortable proportions.

ABOVE The kitchen, which was originally a storeroom, is Stramana's favourite part of the house. Large, airy, and filled with an appealing clutter of saucepans and cooking implements, the room is scented by the dried herbs hanging from its arches.

LEFT The kitchen is a popular spot for serving up easy summer suppers using straightforward Tuscan ingredients—Pecorino cheese, salami and plump ripe tomatoes—served with crusty white bread.

major household events, not just preparing meals. Indeed, stepping into Stramana's own kitchen is like stepping back in time. A worn oak table serves as a work surface, meeting point and supper place; copper pans and cooking utensils are hung on every available surface; and copious bunches of herbs dry from the rafters. Many of the plants are medicinal and are part of Stramana's research for a book she is writing on herbs and memory.

Stramana dedicated herself with equal enthusiasm to the decoration of the interiors, which are relaxed yet elegant and marked by an eclectic assortment of furniture. Some of the furnishings, like the master bed, have followed her from her home in Venice. Others have been acquired in Montepulciano or on frequent forays to other Tuscan towns. A common theme that runs through the house is her love of antique textiles. While many pieces were inherited from her grandmother

ABOVE A handsomely embroidered Arab wedding gown, a present from the brother of King Hussein of Jordan, decorates the entrance to the guest bedroom.

and great-grandmother, others are the result of her continuous collecting.

The family lives here year-round. Once summer arrives, their life shifts from inviting fireplaces to the shady garden. A wide covered portico, originally built to house carriages and farm equipment, is now adapted to use as a summer living room. The garden is simple and Stramana's only intervention was the addition of her beloved herbs, which gently perfume the air on warm afternoons and balmy evenings.

ABOVE & RIGHT In decorating the bedrooms, Stramana has paid great attention to even the smallest detail, whether antique linens and draperies enlivening a wrought-iron bed or a porcelain wash basin and jug.

Inspired Solitude

Some people seek the tranquil country life of Tuscany to escape from work. Others are attracted by the textures and tastes that the area offers up to all who care to linger.

Vibeke Lökkeberg came to this corner of Tuscany to capture all this and more. For in restoring Il Casone, she has created something unique: a retreat tucked away in the Tuscan hills, where she comes to relax, certainly, but also to find the peace and silence necessary for creativity.

Lökkeberg is a Norwegian film director who writes and stars in her own films. While on holiday here ten years ago, she came across this large, rambling, rundown house and decided to sink her roots in this sunny clime, far from home. The house, most of which was built in the last century, was quite large. Although much loved, Il Casone resisted her attentions, and she wasn't quite satisfied with the solutions she had come up with for transforming the ramshackle building. Luckily, neighbours Michele Cantatore (an architect) and Emanuela Stramana (an interior designer) were willing and able to help her rework this farmhouse into a warmly elegant, rural hideaway.

LEFT Simplicity and tranquility characterize the house of Vibeke Lökkeberg.

When not in residence, Lökkeberg often lends the house to friends and colleagues, writers and artists looking for a little solitude and the time to create. The ingenious layout of the house allows a great deal of privacy for both guests and owners. Four independent suites, complete with kitchens, allow visitors to spend whole days without seeing another soul. A spacious living room and outdoor terraces provide opportunities to socialize for those who are willing.

Warm yellows and ochres were used for the interior walls throughout the house. Applied unevenly, these earth tones provide a textured background for the austere lines of rustic furnishings or for canopied beds draped in stiff folds of white linen. Another constant element is the use of handmade terracotta tiles on the floors, broken only by the occasional throw rug. The impression is of uncluttered modernity and provincial comfort, a merging of Tuscan warmth and Scandinavian purity.

The garden surrounding the building has been kept simple. A few oaks provide shade, a handful of rosemary bushes scent the air and scented roses burst into bloom each May. Together, house and garden provide a soothing and unpretentious environment for all those who come to Il Casone to rest, work and find inspiration.

RIGHT Although the house is undeniably rustic in its architectural detail and its building materials, Lökkeberg has endowed it with a modern edge by streamlining the decoration, using simple, robust furnishings, and by keeping the rooms purposefully minimal. The dining room features a solid chestnut table with a marble top.

ABOVE & OPPOSITE Vibeke Lökkeberg's Scandinavian roots are clearly evident in the bathroom, with its scrubbed, wholesome looks and earthy romance. Large-brimmed straw hats stand ready for guests who venture out into the bright Tuscan sunshine.

ABOVE Equally calming is the guest kitchen, with solid country furniture washed in green and scrubbed back to reveal the timber patina.

♡sasha

LEFT In the guest bedroom, the twin beds are given a sophisticated yet pure look with white cotton canopies.

OPPOSITE & ABOVE The master suite, with its canopied bed, drapes and chair covers in bleached desert colours, is as sumptuous as Lökkeberg's spare aesthetic allows. The canopies were designed by her neighbour Emanuela Stramana and give the room a Middle Eastern feel. Other furnishings include a chaise longue covered in deep green velvet and a pair of Oriental rugs, which provide a contrast to the pale walls and drapes.

Organic Forms

Architect Jacques Couëlle had a natural affinity with the rocky curves, grottoes and cliffs of the Riviera coastline. They fit perfectly within his philosophical vision of humankind returning to its cave-dwelling roots. He wanted to create habitats that would return modern men and women to the molten, sculptural feel of the caves they once inhabited, and to produce buildings in synergy with their natural settings. This vision lies at the heart of an extraordinary house in the Baie de Cannes, designed by Couëlle in 1973.

The current owners had experienced the architect's unique view of design and living style while on holiday at the Cala di Volpe Hotel in Sardinia. A luxury resort developed by the Agha Khan and conceived by architect Jacques Couëlle, it springs from the island like an organic rock formation, a

LEFT The primitive, almost timeless quality of Couëlle's vision allows the owners to mix objects and furnishings from different eras with no apparent conflict. In the large drawing room, an antique grandfather clock and the gold cherub suspended above seem perfectly at home.

fluid, living sculpture. The couple were so taken by this enigmatic place that they commissioned Couëlle to execute such a sculpture on the Côte d'Azur.

By this time at the height of his career, Couëlle had developed a fully formed concept for his unique brand of organic architecture. He set about realising his ideas on the clifftop site purchased by the owners, high above the bustle of Cannes. Like other projects the architect had conceived, the house was to be a "floating environment" that was rooted to the land but seemed to be suspended in space. It was to be elegant, but so married to the landscape that it appeared almost invisible.

Couëlle, like all the artists who were attracted to the Côte d'Azur, was fascinated by light and the way it changed the mood and appearance of the interior of a house as it ran its course from morning till evening. The interaction between natural and artificial light was also an important consideration, along with the impact of both light sources on the inhabitant's perception of space, furniture and objets d'art. This is evident in the house at Baie de Cannes, which is sited to capture and filter the changing strengths of the sun throughout the day—illuminating the stuccoed free-forms and fluid arches that delineate the interior space and drawing attention to the breathtaking sea views that punctuate the exterior walls.

The owners found themselves caught up in the spirit of Couëlle's vision, and began to collect artworks and local crafts that would complement the structural beauty of their new home. They acquired everything from

ABOVE & OPPOSITE Architect Jacques Couëlle has created an extraordinary cave-dwelling, Riviera style, for this site overlooking the Mediterranean. Its molten, flowing forms and primitive feel provide an apt backdrop for the owners' collection of modern sculpture.

LEFT & ABOVE This corner of the main living room is a tribute to the regional culture and geography. Behind the curved leather-covered banquette, a wall of niches is filled with all kinds of treasured objects, from shells and sponges and rustic door keys to vivid stained glass and neo-realist art works. Couëlle was very involved in the neo-realist art movement of the 1920s and 1930s, counting Yves Kline among his friends, and he inspired the owners to start collecting.

canvases by Yves Kline and pots by Jean Maret, a good friend and contemporary of Picasso, to Etruscan-inspired vases by Tomek, which are at once classical and contemporary. These objects still decorate the house, which today appears just as avant-garde as it did in 1973. At the same time, however—in keeping with Couëlle's intention—its organic, sculptural qualities make it appear at one with its environment, as if it had slowly evolved from the ground over the course of centuries.

OPPOSITE & ABOVE Better than any museum setting, the Couëlle house boasts sweeping organic forms and a bold interplay of light and shadow that provide a natural showcase for sculpture. A primitive figurine is displayed in a niche framing an exquisite sea view, while a colonnaded walkway is the setting for a collection of vases, inspired by ancient amphora and made by local potters.

ABOVE Although niches apparently occur at random, they have been carefully thought out to be as functional as they are aesthetic. Household and decorative items can be neatly stored, eradicating the need for cupboards and enclosed storage areas.

ABOVE & OPPOSITE The fireplace unit provides one such example, with spaces carved out of the structure to allow for the placement of the fire itself as well for storing logs. Couëlle has created the illusion that a lava flow has poured over the site, forming solid shapes as it cooled. His idea was to create living spaces that would put modern humans back in touch with their roots, returning them to the molten, sculptural feeling of their natural habitats as cave dwellers.

Alpine Dreams

Natural Refuge

In Alpine resorts as popular as the Swiss village of Klosters, it is challenging enough trying to find a suitable home in the town. Near-impossible though is the prospect of acquiring a house in the serene foothills above the town. Planning regulations all but prevent new construction and existing farmhouses tend to be held on to by the families that have lived there for generations. Artist Sonya Knapp is one of the few outsiders who have managed to buy a piece of this mountain paradise for herself.

Knapp was living in a small apartment in a house in the centre of Klosters but craved the isolation and space that a house would bring. Eventually she found a traditional farmhouse chalet for sale high above the valley. On the sunny side of Mount Gotchner, it was to become a haven into which Knapp poured heart and soul.

The house as Knapp found it was a single-storeyed structure dating from 1893, but needed extensive reshaping to create the working home the artist wanted.

OPPOSITE A late-nineteenth century farmhouse on a hill above Klosters was a rare find for artist Sonya Knapp. On top of the house she has built an atelier, using local wood so that the extension blends seamlessly with the original structure.

ABOVE & RIGHT The house is primarily a place for creation, and the artist spends the winter months in the top-floor atelier working on sketches, ink paintings and sculptures. A long stint in Japan influenced not only her artistic style but her living environment as well. In place of curtains, Sonya Knapp has covered windows with paper and bamboo shoji screens, which soften the harsh alpine sunlight.

A second floor was added to give her a large and airy atelier and the existing ground floor was opened out. The restoration was seamless. From the outside the additional floor looks to have been there forever, while inside the use of old timbers retains the integrity of the original house. What makes Knapp's home so intriguing is her artist's eye for colour and her close relationship with the natural environment, including its seasonal changes. The two elements strike a harmonious balance, a quality that is also true of Knapp's art. Canvases in progress in her atelier and finished works on the walls of the house show the artist's talent for recording nature in her own stylized way, whether floral motifs or her favourite subject, black cats.

The decoration of the house was a collaborative effort with friend and colleague Emmanuel Ungaro. He chose mainly seventeenth- and eighteenth-century English antique furnishings for their sense of solidity and because the darker wood echoed the aged timber of the interior walls and ceilings. Having previously designed fabrics for Ungaro, Knapp shared the fashion designer's passion for colour and floral themes. They used bright kilims

LEFT & ABOVE Natural materials inspire the artist—outside wooden animals from Nepal create a whimsical menagerie. The house is intended to adapt to the changing seasons. In summer, sofas and chairs are covered in plain white and the rooms filled with fresh flowers. In winter, however, it is designed to give an impression of warmth, with rich colours and bold patterns defining the living area, a legacy of the artist's work with designer Ungaro. Sonya Knapp is known for her stylish yet poignant ink paintings of flowers and animals, especially cats, which she finds the most challenging subjects.

ABOVE & RIGHT In the entrance hall, a big cat rendered in ink chases a sculptural bird. Both pieces are by Sonya Knapp. Below the stairs, dried hydrangeas, a lamp with rose-like stem, an antique cuckoo clock and one of the artist's framed pastels form one of of many still-life settings around floral themes.

on the floors to add warmth and hunted out antique fabrics to cover sofas and cushions. Time spent in Japan inspired the sliding windows lined with shoji paper—designed to soften the strong Alpine light and eradicate the need for heavy curtains. The Japanese mood is also felt in the owner's keen affinity with seasonal changes, and use of images derived from nature.

During winter, pretty floral prints cover sofas and chairs, while bunches of dried flowers add the bright touches Knapp feels are essential in a mountain home during winter. All this changes in the summer, though, when chair coverings are swapped for plain white upholstery and the only flowers to be seen are fresh ones. With the outdoors ablaze with brilliant greens, the interior looks fresh and clean—a symbolic breath of new life reflecting the changing natural world.

Winter Solace

Klosters has a reputation for being one of the most rustic of the Swiss resorts. Quiet, and with a strong sense of the farming village it still is, Klosters is what the locals might call *gemütlich*—cosy, warm and welcoming. It is this quality that attracts an entourage of semi-permanent residents, who live elsewhere but have maintained a base here for years, a place of escape used throughout the year. There are few, though, who can claim shares in such a special piece of the resort's architectural heritage.

Eva Beckwith has a long association with Klosters. She has been coming to the town since she was nine years old, and has always had a home of some kind here. However, the one house she longed for, and walked past everyday for years seemed always out of her reach. An early seventeenth-century farmhouse set a few minutes walk from the town centre, yet surrounded by fields, it has been in the hands of one longtime Klosters farming family for more than a century. The problem is that properties such as these rarely become available to outsiders. When Beckwith heard that this particular house might be for rent she jumped at the chance to pursue it. She knew immediately that here she could create the

LEFT Although just a five-minute walk away from the centre of Klosters, the farmhouse stands in the middle of a field. In winter, a short trek across the field leads to excellent cross-country tracks.

LEFT & OPPOSITE A simple farmhouse table and bench seats form the centrepiece of the kitchen. At one end is an eighteenth-century chestnut larder from the Le Marche area of Italy, now used to store crockery and utensils. Eva Beckwith's restrained decorative style creates wonderfully atmospheric rooms like the dining room with its French wrought iron candelabra.

perfect weekend base for regular escapes from the cashmere business she runs in Zurich. The space offered for rental was a large apartment on the first floor of the house, which had been converted in 1914 to provide separate living quarters for the farmer's family and his mother.

It was to be another few years, however, before Beckwith could take possession of the old farmhouse. With sagging floors and a thick layer of dirt over everything, the house was in serious need of work. Beckwith, an interior decorator, offered to help the owners with the crucial renovations. The ancient timber floors—hanging, with no under-support—were to prove the most challenging aspect. Each of the floorboards was removed, iron beams inserted at floor level to provide a stable framework, and then each of the old boards

ABOVE & RIGHT The sitting room is cocooned by pale honey-coloured wood that lines the ceiling, walls and floor. Furnishings have been kept low-key, focusing the attention on a few special objects and works of art including the original green porcelain kachelofen, *or tile stove, and a Balinese painting from Ubud. The sitting room of this seventeenth-century farmhouse apartment conveys a sense of ease, without the usual clutter of traditional alpine decoration. The owner has evolved a look reminiscent of British colonial homes.*

ABOVE & OPPOSITE The master bedroom derives its charm from the unpretentious furnishing with a Balinese wicker chair, an Italian appliqué bedcover and the colonial style accessories such as the sun hats on the wall.

cleaned and put back in place. New electrical circuits and plumbing were installed with full central heating.

Even after Beckwith had moved in and decorated the farmhouse apartment, there was still one massive job to be carried out—restoring the parquetry floor in the study. Created from alternating squares of pale elm and dark maple, the chequerboard floor had become coated with layers of dirt over the years, obscuring the colour and grain of the wood. The owner of the house himself carried out the delicate operation of removing each square, numbering it, then cleaning it and returning it to the same spot. This elegant flooring seems unlikely decor for a farmhouse, but it was not uncommon for wealthy farmers to have one special room for receiving guests. It now serves as the study, while the main sitting room is more relaxed, decorated with comfortable sofas and artworks and objects acquired on travels abroad. But the effect is far from cluttered. Although the rooms are infused with touches of old-world charm and hints of colonial informality, a modern restraint pervades the entire house, and the sense of internal space is never sacrificed.

LEFT Encircled by fir trees, swathed in a thick blanket of snow and seemingly isolated, the house takes on an enchanted quality during the winter months.

Natural Clarity

On a rare plot of land in St Moritz, a modern experiment in mountain living is underway. Few residents of Switzerland's first resort have the luxury of starting from scratch on a pristine site in an exclusive residential area. It is skirted by forest, traversed by a stream for fishing in summer and situated at the base of the Corviglio ski run, so that in winter and early spring a day's skiing begins and ends at the front door.

For Bruno and Bettina Müller and their two young daughters, this enviable location was the starting point for a holiday home planned with architectural precision. At the beginning of their search for a home in St Moritz, they engaged architect Arnd Küchel, who not only found the land but laid down the blueprint for the house and oversaw both its construction and interior fit-out. Family friend and renowned Italian designer Antonio Citterio

RIGHT A Tricia Guild tulip print covers the armchairs in one corner of the living room, an extension of the red and white theme. The Müllers have built a wooden bird house on the small terrace as a feeding spot for birds from the forest. As many as thirty birds at a time cluster here during winter, and bright yellow cut-outs deter the birds from flying into the glass.

LEFT The traditional Swiss colours of red and white are given a modern twist in the loft-like living room with its pale ceiling of larch. The interior was not highly planned but evolved from the simple idea of a large white sofa scattered with checked flanelette cushions, which forms the centrepiece of the room.

OPPOSITE Designed to be at one with its environment, the Müller house is constructed from regional granite and timber. Using these traditional materials architect Arnd Küchel created a modern house in the midst of 3,000 square metres of forest.

also lent his expertise to the project, and his influence is evident in the beautiful simplicity of the house and the attention to detail.

The client brief was that the house should be built of natural materials to harmonize with the environment, and that the very layout would enable the inhabitants to feel instantly at one with nature outside—to feel that the house was interacting with nature. Küchel devised a house built of regional stone that comprised a three-storey tower and a connecting L-shaped wing. In the tower are a children's playroom on the ground floor, master bedroom on the level above and living room on the top level. The adjoining wing contains three bedrooms, each with its own bathroom. Each section of the house was designed in such a way as to look directly outside to either the natural forest adjoining the property, the mountains or the garden.

Unusually for a cold-climate house, the ceilings are high and the windows are huge, with virtually no curtaining at all, This allows uninhibited views and gives the impression that nothing stands between the viewer and the scenic beauty beyond. The one concession to practicality is sturdy exterior wooden shutters that can seal off windows from outside elements if necessary. Even the chimney flue for the fireplace in the living room has been suspended from the ceiling and stands before a plate glass window looking out at the fir trees. Even this most essential alpine feature has been made subservient to the natural beauty outside.

To give an impression of warmth to the large-scale interiors, reddish-gold larch wood was used for floors and for beamed ceilings, while creamy-white stucco veneziano on the walls provides a neutral backdrop for occasional strokes of colour—like the red in the living room, or bright lavender blue in the master bedroom.

As much as possible though, the room decor was purposely restrained, and the overall effect

OPPOSITE & LEFT The master bedroom appears to be nestled in the bough of the fir trees just outside. From the low bed, the couple can look out into the forest. Decoration has been kept to a functional minimum. A far cry from the cosy clutter of a typical Swiss alpine kitchen, the Müllers cooking and eating area is streamlined and fuss-free, with an appealing Scandinavian simplicity. The focus of attention is the view across the valley to the mountains.

is one of striking simplicity. With the exception of a few key pieces of modern art, there are few other distractions: no collections of local woodcarving on display, no pewter tankards, no antique memorabilia or knick-knacks—only essential furnishings and lighting. The idea is that nature provides all the aesthetic enhancement needed for this elementary yet highly evolved mountain residence.

LEFT Snowy expanses surround the farmhouse during the winter months, allowing the owner plenty of opportunities for skiing and snow-shoeing.

Farmhouse Retreat

Alpine wood, cut from the pines of the Dolomites, has been used to build chalets in Cortina for hundreds of years. Its warm, golden-brown hue and aged patina are almost impossible to replicate with modern building materials. Much of it was stripped from chalets and farmhouses during the 1950s and 1960s when they were converted into modern flats. As a result, this antique wood has become highly prized by home owners in the resort, many of whom have gone to great lengths to acquire it from an old house about to be demolished, transferring it length by length to its adopted home.

Only a dozen or so residents in Cortina are fortunate enough to live in properties untouched by modernization. Publisher Leonardo Mondadori is one of them, and he is not blind to his good fortune—perhaps because he spent two decades waiting for it. Mondadori has been visiting Cortina regularly since the age of two. He was twenty-five when he first saw the house that was to eventually become his mountain retreat. He mentally earmarked it as his own, but it was not until some twenty years later that his ski instructor introduced him to a friend who suggested a way to make his dream reality.

ABOVE & RIGHT The original stove has been retained in a corner of the dining room, making it one of the warmest spots in the house. In times past, the platform above the stove provided a place for sleeping. The master bedroom is encased in antique knotted pine. Almost filling the bedroom is an exquisitely panelled fifteenth-century gothic bed, which had to be reassembled in the room piece by piece.

The large eighteenth-century farmhouse stands on the outskirts of town, commanding views across the valley to Mount Tofana. Owned by the church—a gift from a parishioner who died without heirs—it was close to ruin, but the church lacked the funds to fix it. Mondadori approached the parish officials with an offer they couldn't refuse—he would undertake the costly task of fully restoring the property in return for a long lease granting him right of residency.

When beginning work on the house, the first priority was to prevent its imminent collapse. A

LEFT & ABOVE A formal dining room now occupies the former feed stalls for the farm animals. The table and fourteen chairs were designed in provincial style to suit the rustic quality of the room. The horn chandelier was found in an antique shop near Cortina. Leonardo Mondadori is an avid collector of pottery, ceramics and rustic utensils. In the kitchen they strike just the right note, adding interest without compromising the beautiful austerity of the room.

team of craftsmen then spent two years restoring and rebuilding every feature, from the roof to the floorboards. In order to re-use the original interior wood, every plank was dismantled, cleaned and then reassembled. Once the structure had been completely refurbished, Mondadori turned to its decoration, commissioning Rome-based interior designer Verdi Visconti. With its large, wood-lined rooms and massive beamed ceilings, the house had such a strong personality that it required decorating with a restrained hand. Visconti concentrated on solid, streamlined furnishings, modern blocks of colour, discreet

OPPOSITE & ABOVE The historic house has such a strong personality that owner Leonardo Mondadori wanted to keep all decoration to a minimum. He has even retained the original layout of the house, one of the few in Cortina to have survived intact for several centuries. The wood lining the walls and ceiling of this sitting room has also survived—its rich patina required little embellishment to create a cosy place for informal meals.

OPPOSITE & ABOVE The bathrooms are charmingly earthy in character. The handcrafted wooden bathtub was inspired by traditional Japanese o-furo.

lighting and monumental pieces of art to achieve the desired effect. She avoided the romantic patterning and heavily textured Tirolean-style interior so typical elsewhere in Cortina.

The end result of Visconti's considered eye and Mondadori's unpretentious tastes is a house of great character. It has an eclectic quality that accommodates both the rough and refined. Uneven stone walls and smoothly polished floors, Julian Schnabel canvases and provincial ceramics, farmhouse furniture and Mondadori's own extraordinary handmade Gothic bed sit together with equal ease. None of these disparate elements, however, distract from the integrity of the historic structure itself.

LEFT The hay loft is now a relaxed, open living room for entertaining friends. The idea was to create a welcoming space that was not in the least bit imposing. Low seating areas were formed with soft, crimson wool sofas that are more like mattresses in style.

ERIC
The Six
Books
Diadem

OPPOSITE A large, south-facing dining room offers panoramic views of Aspen's mountains. The interior is partially lined with spruce, emitting a sweet subtle smell that infuses the cabin with the scent of the woods outside.

Cabin Fever

On the south side of Aspen mountain, on what its owner describes as one of the most beautiful sites in America, is a property that follows in the tradition of the mountain shelters of Alpine Europe. It is a small chalet, built by hand using timber and stone from the surrounding land by local architect Wayne Poulsen. Most of his work has been done in mountain settings and his expertise in designing structures attuned to their location is evident here.

Poulsen spent four years building his cabin by hand out of massive logs cut from spruce trees on the ten-acre site, which was once a mining claim. All his experience in mountain architecture and his passion for Aspen's ski country have gone into it. It is built in the style of a late-nineteenth-century Swiss chalet. But unlike the wooden chalets of Switzerland with their neat windows encased by shutters, Poulsen's house incorporates vast walls of glass looking out onto a pristine, sun-drenched mountain landscape. The wonderfully temperate Aspen climate, with bright skies through most of the winter months, means that more heat is trapped by allowing the sun into the house than is lost through the expanses of glass. This feature also gives the home a strong connection with its wild and isolated setting.

Inside, the cabin is simple and comfortable, dominated by the solid spruce logs and their subtly sweet aroma. They form a canopy over the large main room, which comprises a south-facing living area with adjoining dining space and kitchen. A bedroom, bathroom and sleeping loft complete the compact mountain retreat. It is furnished in a sturdy Alpine style. A giant sleigh bed that provides fireside seating and the long dining table is made from solid logs joined in classic Alpine fashion.

The 1,000-square foot cabin provides ample space for Poulsen's weekend ski getaways. A twenty-minute drive along a dirt road that winds up the back side of Aspen Mountain carries him from his main home and architectural practice in Aspen to his chalet door. Once a miner's

LEFT & ABOVE Architect Wayne Poulsen built his cabin himself, from logs hewn from trees that had fallen or died on the surrounding acreage. He was inspired by the traditional art of building mountain shelters.

ABOVE, LEFT & OPPOSITE *When friends arrive for mid-week ski parties or weekend soirées, they gather around the huge fireplace, perching on fireside cushions or curling up on the Norwegian-*

style sleigh bed. The galleried loft upstairs provides ample sleeping space. During summer, the grand piano takes pride of place when Poulsen hosts his own private music festival.

access track, the road can only be navigated by snowcat during the long winter months. A short foray further up the mountain puts Poulsen directly on the piste.

Although originally intended as an upscale ski hut providing instant access to the slopes, it has become much more. Poulsen often finds himself here during the week, just to spend the day, or to cook dinner for friends. The enormous French-style central fireplace is put to service for informal suppers, prepared on a grill over the open fire, and if guests want to stay over, there is plenty of room in the galleried sleeping loft. In summer, when the cultural activities in town are in full swing, Poulsen hosts a private piano festival, performing on his grand piano and inviting friends

OPPOSITE, ABOVE & LEFT *As the cabin is often used for entertaining, most of the space is given over to an open-plan kitchen and dining area. To make the most of the views, the cabin was designed with unusually large windows. Aspen is fairly southern in location and its winter sun quite strong—therefore the heat coming through the windows more than compensates for any heat lost through the expanses of glass. Since the cabin can be reached in only twenty minutes from Aspen by snowmobile, it is a perfect starting point for day-trips into the mountains on skis.*

to play. Despite the undoubted charms of the cabin in summer, when wildflowers carpet the fields outside and the sky stays light until late into the evening, the chalet really comes into its own in winter when the vast snowy landscape outside serves only to emphasize the warmth of the fire inside and the gentle scent of spruce that fills the cabin.

LEFT All of the materials used to build the house were found in the area. Much of the timber was from the old mine shafts around Aspen, while stones came from the river bed. The house was constructed almost singlehandedly by its visionary creator.

Native Habitat

Curled like a giant Nautilus shell on the snowy fringes of Aspen's Buttermilk Run is the extraordinary house of Peter and Patricia Findlay. It is a wholly organic structure in both its layout and materials. Built mostly from river bed stone and wood, the house is set into the earth so that from certain angles it appears virtually imbedded in it, completely at one with the open land around it. Inside, all the rooms sweep into a central open space that rises through the three levels of the house. There are no rendered walls or conventional building treatments: all the surfaces are left rough and raw, and spaces simply flow into each other.

The highly unconventional design and execution of the house were what drew the Findlays to it when they came to Aspen looking for a holiday home. After scouring the town without finding what they wanted, they saw the property advertised, accompanied only by photographs of the expansive views it commanded. Their curiosity piqued, they persuaded a reluctant estate agent to show it to them, despite his best efforts to convince them it would be a waste of time. It was precisely because the house was so unusual that it had failed to attract buyers in the past, in spite its having been on the market for several years. The Findlays, however, immediately appreciated its individualistic character and decided it was a treasure worth owning. They saw it not only as wonderful example of organic architecture but as a slice of Aspen's modern history.

The house is a shrine to 1970s counterculture — so much so that it is known to everyone locally as 'the mushroom house' in reference to the magic mushrooms to which its original owner was apparently partial. He was one of many who came to

Aspen in the 1960s and 1970s in search of an alternative lifestyle and a creative environment in tune with nature. He set his mind to building his own house with his own hands, using materials he found in the region. He hauled tons of stone from the river to form the basis for his hippie haven and delved down into the old mine sites to heave up timber beams, which he used for the roof and for structural and interior details. Furnishings were low and casual, often built-in, in keeping with the style of the decade.

So neatly did all the elements of the house fit together that the Findlays have changed little about it. Although they have added a few decorative touches of their own here and there, the rest is largely as it was. The circular lounge area features a built-in sofa, still covered in its original fabric. The dining room retains the hanging glass light fitting made especially for the room in the 1970s. Original fireplaces, cut like gashes into the stone walls, and randomly placed stained-glass windows have all stayed in tact.

ABOVE & OPPOSITE When the Findlays took over the house, the interior resembled a jungle, literally dripping with greenery. The couple removed much of the vegetation in order to simplify and open up the interior space. They have kept just a few potted palms and hanging ferns to give the impression that the house is a living, breathing organism.

FOLLOWING SPREAD This organically designed house owes much to the alternative culture of the 1970s in both its earthy forms and its surreal visual quality. It curls like a nautilus shell from an inner core out into the open living area.

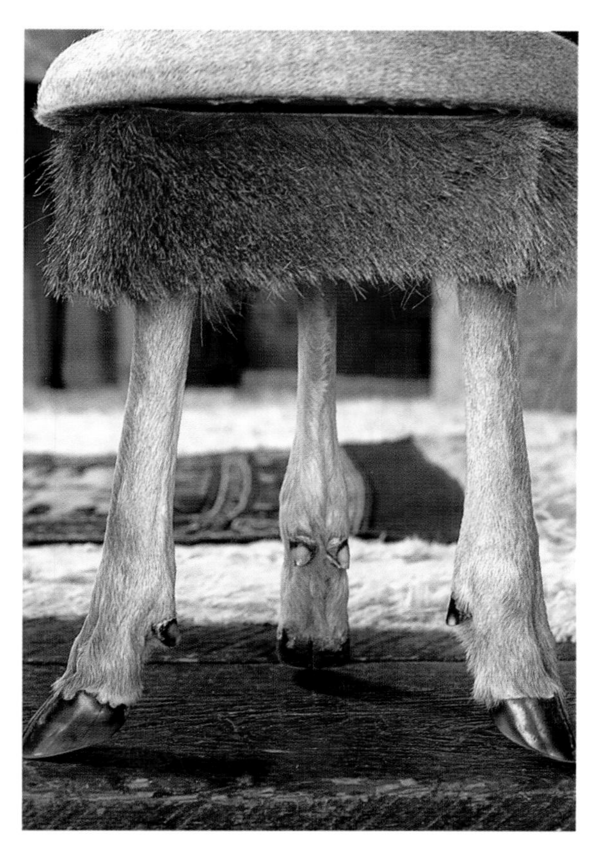

LEFT & ABOVE The fireplace in the main living area is constructed from a welded unit suspended inside the stone wall, with vents on each floor to disperse the heat. It is indicative of the alternative approach to living embodied in the house. The downstairs sitting room is lined in river bed stone. Low-level seating is clustered beside a massive fireplace which generates an enormous amount of heat. An old pair of snowshoes hangs on one wall.

Most spectacularly of all, the master bedroom has been kept as its creator intended: fitted with a giant circular waterbed that almost fills the whole room, with only a small surrounding ledge for access. A panel of large windows in the curving exterior wall and a huge skylight overhead mean the sky, stars, trees and mountains can be viewed languidly from bed. No magic mushrooms are needed to make this a truly surreal experience.

LEFT & ABOVE Sheltered from behind by Smuggler Mountain, the house is nestled in a sun trap and is bathed in light for most of the day. Holly Lueders uses the sun-drenched terrace as her studio, even in winter. In the event of bad weather, a long covered walkway rises from ground level to the entrance to ensure safe passage from the car to the house.

Pioneer Spirit

The home of artist and interior designer Holly Lueders pays homage to the spirit of pioneering America. The lodge is in no way nostalgic; rather, the use of raw, rugged materials and an organic approach to decoration give the house its character. Poised on the south face of Smuggler Mountain in Aspen's North Star Preserve, surrounded by a snowy wilder-

OPPOSITE, ABOVE & RIGHT Looking out over the Roaring Fork River, which snakes its way through Aspen's North Star Preserve, the house of artist Holly Lueders is designed to harmonize with its environment of snowy mountain wilderness. The massive logs used to construct the house were hewn from fallen trees in Yellowstone and Vail National Parks. Offering a natural form of insulation, they are so thick, that very little in the way of heating is required inside. Although the family have other homes, they choose to spend the winters here. Most days between January and March find them out cross-country or downhill skiing. When they stay here during the summer, their energies are chanelled into cycling and fishing.

ABOVE & RIGHT Beautiful and unusual objects are woven into the rugged framework of the house, like a delicate etched-glass chandelier. Decorative tiles are another a key element in the interior design of the main living areas. In the library, reproduction tiles from the Henry Mercer tileworks in Pennsylvania surround the fireplace, telling the story of Rip Van Winkle.

LEFT & ABOVE The vast 'great room' is the focus for family life. Lueders set out to create a space where all could be together, yet do their own thing. The result is numerous cosy seating areas.

ness, Lueders' winter retreat blends seamlessly with its environment.

Affectionately dubbed North Star Lodge by its owner, the house is certainly on the scale of a lodge, stretched out across the mountain's foothills, an expansive two storey structure, capped by four pitched roofs and with a deep veranda running the length of the facade. This expansive outdoor deck serves as Lueders' studio and workroom, where even winter mornings are spent working on the handcrafted tole trays and ceramics for which she is known.

The exterior and internal structures are of solid logs cut from dead or fallen trees harvested locally or from Yellowstone. Up to eighteen inches thick, these logs provide natural insulation from the elements. They also enable the luxury of picture windows, which run from floor to roofline offering views to the preserve and the Roaring Fork River which cuts through it.

Even inside, the fabric of nature is ever-present: walls lined with bark, a feature wall of lichen rock, chandeliers of elk antlers, and beds from tree branches.

RIGHT & OPPOSITE Throughout the house cosy sofas, cushions, upholstered stools and carpets contrast nicely with the rough surfaces of wood and stone. The mosaic backgammon table sets an interesting accent.

Texture is everything in Lueders' domain. She employed decorative artists and artisans to work on almost every aspect of the interior fittings and furniture. In cladding the walls with bark or setting beams or railings, they selected and placed the timbers so that interesting knots or features of the wood would be seen and appreciated.

Comfort and decoration are just as important to Lueders as the rough materials drawn from the mountains around her. This counterpoint gives the house great charm and reinforces the idea of it as a modern frontier refuge. When early nineteenth-century pioneers to the Wild West built log homes using massive pine trees cut from the woods, they gave them homely touches with colourful quilts, hand-embroidered throws and delicately patterned textiles. In the same vein, Lueders has introduced colour and pattern to make her lodge a place of warmth and natural artfulness.

Ceramics are a key element at North Star Lodge—symbolic perhaps of the meeting between rough and smooth, of the

NORTHSTAR

OPPOSITE & ABOVE The house incorporates eight bedrooms, each with a bed crafted from fallen trees found on the property. In contrast to the gnarled branches that form the bed bases and sculptural bedheads, hand-embroidered spreads and cushions made from Hungarian felted wool provide touches of warmth, colour and comfort.

interplay between raw elements and aesthetic concerns that characterize this home. Lueders' passion for the ceramic arts led her to commission special pieces from the Doylestown, Pennsylvania tileworks designed by Henry Mercer, the innovative collector and ceramicist of the 1920s, using Mercer's original moulds. In the kitchen, the artist's New World tiles bear images of the folktales and natural environment of North and South America. Around the library fireplace, other tiles convey visually the narrative of Rip Van Winkle, the ceramic surfaces smoked and oiled to give them a patina of age. Elsewhere, young tile artisans from all over the country have supplied works for Lueders' paean to American craftsmanship.

ABOVE & RIGHT One of two master bedroom suites that Holly Lueders and her husband switch between, depending on the season. The walls are lined with bark, which was picked in spring and pressed for six months before being fitted. The fireplace, with its mosaic of wood patterns and textures, is a monument to the craftsmen of the Rocky Mountains and their ability to translate indigineous materials into works of art.

ABOVE & OPPOSITE A snow-white bedroom that reflects the landscape outside. The bed, like the others in the house, was commissioned from a local artisan to give the illusion that the natural world had found its way inside. In fact, most of ~~the~~ furnishings are handcrafted, including a rustic armchair made from willow.

On the Emerald Isle

Community Spirit

Cill Rialaig is a mere cluster of tiny stone cottages, one of the furthermost points of habitation in County Kerry on the west coast of Ireland. Clinging to the edge of the cliff on Bolus Head high above the Atlantic Ocean and Ballin-skelligs Bay, the eleven cottages which make up this isolated hamlet were built about 1790 and have withstood the relentless pounding of the elements through the centuries as rain and winds have gradually taken their toll.

The landscape is beautiful, rugged and demanding. The rocky terrain and spectacular cliffs, with views out to Scariff Island and the distant Skelligs, are resonant of an early mysticism which encouraged many to seek out this wild, unforgiving countryside and pit themselves against it. A line of megaliths leading up to Bolus Head and the ruins of a hermitage beyond the village stand testimony to those who went before.

Yet there are also survivors from the days when Cill Rialaig was still a struggling community. A glimpse of Mrs Kelly, comfort-able in the passenger seat of a modern jeep as she is ferried to the local town a good distance away, brings the story right up to date for she was the last to vac-

LEFT The Iveragh Peninsula of County Kerry which extends into the Atlantic Ocean is one of the remotest stretches of European coastline, where the extreme weather conditions and high seas batter the cliffs in a daily confrontation.

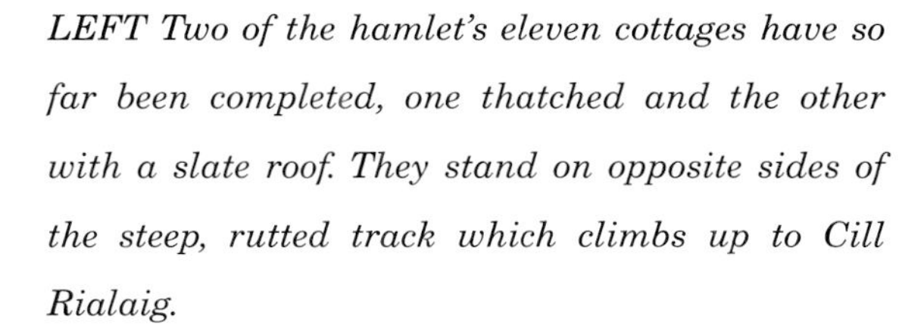

LEFT Two of the hamlet's eleven cottages have so far been completed, one thatched and the other with a slate roof. They stand on opposite sides of the steep, rutted track which climbs up to Cill Rialaig.

ABOVE The rugged exterior of Noelle's house, which was restored and adapted by architect Alfred Cochrane. The idea was to retain the original stone walls and remain as true as possible to the vernacular architecture of the area.

ABOVE & RIGHT The views from Cill Rialaig's remote coastline are spectacular, whether toward the ruins of a keep or across Ballinskelligs Bay towards Scariff Island. A peat fire next to a small cast-iron oven warms Noelle's cosy sitting room.

ate the hamlet back in the 1950s. Now she lives in a modern bungalow as close as possible to her old home, which, like so many of the other cottages, finally descended into ruin. But recently, Mrs Kelly has witnessed the unthinkable—the extraordinary restoration of her village by Noelle Campbell-Sharp, a successful publisher from Dublin, under the sensitive stewardship of friend and architect Alfred Cochrane.

The latest chapter in Cill Rialaig's fascinating history began when Noelle first visited the area over a decade ago and, like many before her, was captivated by the view and the stubborn tenacity

of its inhabitants. Not far from the hamlet she bought a pair of old ruined cottages and cowshed from two elderly sisters, who agreed to sell only after she promised to respect their simple vernacular architecture. As Noelle's own house began to take shape, she found herself becoming increasingly involved with the local community and absorbed with the idea of rekindling life in the abandoned clifftop village. With the help of friends, a small Lottery grant and a wealth of enthusiasm,

ABOVE & OPPOSITE The studio of the Slate House is heated with a cast-iron stove. Paintings by Russia's best-known contemporary artist, Alex Prostov-Pokrovski, line the walls, a legacy of his stay at Cill Rialaig. At one end of the sitting room, a wall paying tribute to what locals refer to as 'keeping holes' is used for storing books. A ladder leads up to a sleeping loft.

Noelle bought the collection of tumbledown cottages in 1991, and with Alfred Cochrane has been gradually restoring them. The purpose behind Noelle's project was to create a new and thriving artistic community at Cill Rialaig, drawing on the unique spirit of the hamlet to attract artists and writers to spend a month at a time in relative isolation in one of the cottages, where they can work without being disturbed. In exchange for this unusual accommodation, which is offered without charge, each artist leaves behind something which he or she have produced during the month of their sojourn. This can then be sold to raise funds to continue the restoration work. The idea has proved extremely popular; the unique quality of light in this far-flung outpost of Ireland is attracting artists of international repute to take up Noelle's offer of hospitality.

ABOVE & RIGHT A decorative late-Victorian fireplace at the end of the bed appears an unusually elegant feature in so isolated a cottage. Noelle's bedroom is decorated in pale shades of blue. A rustic patchwork quilt covers the bed, swirling blue watercolours decorate the walls and pale saris filter the northern light that streams in through small windows.

Whether there will ever be sufficient funds to restore the entire village is a moot point. However, Noelle's efforts to date have been greeted with enthusiastic support by the locals. As guest of honour at a party to celebrate the completion of the first two cottages one summer's evening, Mrs Kelly recalled the last time she had had cause to dance in the village—when a barrel of rum came in on the waves over sixty years ago.

Farm Cottage

A thin spiral of smoke drifts from the stone chimney of the larger of two cottages tucked away against the darkness of the hill. The small yard, enclosed by a dry stone wall, is green with dripping moss, and the neighbouring fields are cropped by sheep. The ground on this still winter's day is hard and unyielding after last night's freeze. It is a perfect day for shooting.

As the sounds of gunfire carry across the hill, preparations for lunch are well underway in the main cottage. A delicious smell of lamb stew wafts from the stove, combining with the unmistakable scent of peat from the fireplace in the living room. Here, a long wooden table has been simply laid for the shooting party, which interrupts the quiet pastoral scene in a long trailer pulled by a noisy tractor, accompanied by a team of excited, if exhausted dogs. As the men gather around the table and the first bottle is broached, conversation turns to the quality of the morning's bag. The host of today's shoot, Hugh O'Neill, draws up a chair to the peat fire, much as all those years ago the last owner of this farm, Jimmy Mann, might have done, warming his outstretched hands.

Old Jimmy Mann, as he was known to Hugh when a boy, is remembered as a rather spooky

LEFT After the main cottage was built, the byre dwelling nearby was used to house the animals.

ABOVE & RIGHT Typical of other such rural Irish properties, a dry stone wall encircles the farmstead. The decoration of the cottage is little changed a few simple objects line the long wooden shelf above the fire.

character, permanently dressed in a black suit and wearing a black hat pulled down low over his face. Mann's Farm represents a typical slice of social and economic history in north Antrim—a tiny farm of no more than fourteen acres and originally part of the O'Neill estates until it was bought out by the Land Acts about 1870. The Mann family would probably have been tenants.

The small stone cottage was the original building on the farm and dates from the sixteenth century. It was known as a byre dwelling: the family would have lived and slept in the loft, and cooked over the open peat fire among the animals on the stone floor below. The earliest survey of 1830 already shows the existence of the second, much larger dwelling and it seems extraordinary that such a small piece of land could have supported the luxury of two dwellings. Despite the presence of the larger cottage, life on the farm was extremely simple, even in Jimmy Mann's time. Meals

LEFT & ABOVE Peat from the bogs fuels the fire in the main parlour, where a table has been laid for lunch, its warmth welcoming the shooting party in from the surrounding woods.

were cooked over the fire, and a dark pot of soup and potatoes was a permanent fixture above the smoking peat. The farm produced flax and potatoes and probably supported a cow and a handful of sheep.

Old Jimmy Mann died intestate and for twelve years or more the farm was abandoned. By this time a near ruin, it was eventually sold to Hugh O'Neill, to whose family estate it had once belonged, and who had always loved its situation and the childhood memories associated with it. Hugh became involved with the Tourist Board in 1986 and

LEFT The byre dwelling has been sensitively restored and the interior transformed into an imaginative bedroom with a gallery. A peat fire is an almost constant feature of the original stone fireplace and chimney.

realised that, unlike Scotland and Wales, Northern Ireland did not cater for holiday cottage lettings. To sell the idea to the local sceptics, Hugh restored Mann's Farm as a prototype, leaving the beamed ceiling and peat fire in the main living room, converting bedrooms under the eaves, and replacing Old Jimmy Mann's unused parlour with a modern kitchen and a bathroom. The original byre dwelling was converted into a wonderfully romantic bedroom with a peat fire. The small wooden door opens out onto the yard and uninterrupted views over to the foothills of Slemish Mountain. Thanks in part to Hugh's sensi-

ABOVE The farm cottages open out onto a yard, enclosed by a dry stone wall, with unhindered views to Slemish Mountain.

tive conversion, there are over 100 cottages which now participate in the letting scheme. With shooting parties during the winter months and tourists through the short summer, Mann's Farm is rarely empty nowadays. Would Old Jimmy Mann recognise his home if he ever returned?

Castle Keep

Sean Ryan plays the penny whistle. A combination of traditional Irish music and his own haunting compositions, whether accompanied by friends in local bars or at ceilidhs, has gained him an international reputation as a musician. His head is filled with stories which have been passed down over the centuries in the form of songs, the old-fashioned way of keeping in touch with the local heritage of which the Irish are so fiercely proud. His wife Anne is a well-known Irish dancer and their daughter Ciara is following in her mother's footsteps.

As a family, the Ryans are touched with a romantic streak, a love of old buildings, and a fascination with the sense of history and untold tales locked within their thick walls. The family was renovating an old Church of Ireland rectory when a rumour reached them that nearby Leap Castle was to be put up for sale. They had barely a day to make up their minds before the property officially came onto the market. Anne had always wanted a castle, but what they bought was a ruin on a massive scale, a restoration project which will probably take them the rest of their lives to complete.

LEFT The Leap of O'Banan (Leim-ui-Bhanain) was an ancient stronghold of the O'Carroll chieftains. Legend is divided as to the origin of its name. Popular local myth relates that two brothers came upon a rocky outcrop and decided that whoever survived after leaping to the ground far below should build a fortress.

The Leap stands sentinel on the border between the counties of Offaly and Tipperary, looking out over rich farmland and a river valley to the Slieve Bloom Mountains beyond. In the gathering gloom of early evening it has a forbidding air, the crenellated walls which surround the property overgrown with grass and ivy. The keep is an ominous black silhouette. One of two Gothic wings which were added in the mid-eighteenth century has tumbled into ruin, its walls blackened by fire.

The Ryans have moved mountains since they first became involved with The Leap, restoring the castle by slow degrees as time and money have afforded. Little remained of the stone floors, windows and doors of the structure, indiscriminately looted over the decades for use on other properties. It took two years just to dig through the rubble and remove the tenacious ivy which had invaded the interior, a voyage of discovery which revealed intimate details about the keep's original structure. Further research in books and old archives from neighbouring Birr Castle has enabled Sean to reconstruct the floors and staircases of the keep, fit Gothic windows and even build a massive baronial fireplace in the entrance hall, reputed to have been one of the grandest in Ireland.

A library in the surviving Georgian wing is well underway, and plans for a huge kitchen with storage rooms in the vaulted

ABOVE & OPPOSITE Leap Castle as it is today, and as it was in its heyday, in an engraving entitled 'The Leap, Seat of Admiral Sir Henry DE Darby KCB'. Upstairs, on the first floor of the central keep, the main reception room is filled by a large refectory table where banquets are held. A daybed at one end of the room, scattered with colourful Indonesian cushions, has been fashioned from wooden panelling that was salvaged from the stables at nearby Birr Castle.

AC
1998
CCR

ABOVE & OPPOSITE In the gathering gloom of a winter's afternoon, ravens settle into the trees which have grown up through the remains of one of the castle's eighteenth-century Gothic-style wings. A baronial fireplace dominates the vast entrance hall, where a new stone floor has been laid around the few remaining slabs of the original structure.

basement have also been drawn up. As yet there are neither bedrooms nor bathrooms, and until the castle is properly habitable, the Ryans have chosen to live in the small, cosy gatehouse.

No medieval castle can be without at least one ghost. Indeed, as Sean started to rebuild the keep he was conscious of being observed by unseen eyes and sometimes felt another presence in the room. Two little girls in period dress, thought to be from the Darby family who once lived in the castle, are The Leap's most permanent other-worldly visitors and have been seen on several occasions—the elder of the two sisters, Emily, is known to have fallen from the battlements in the early seventeenth century.

With the Ryans as the custodians of Leap Castle's future, it has become a favourite location

for organized tours of reputedly haunted houses in Ireland. Banquets and evenings of music are laid on in the keep during the summer feasts for visiting Americans, during which suckling pig and game are roasted over the hall fire, and ghostly spirits mingle with those of the living as stories unfold down the long refectory table.

ABOVE & OPPOSITE An Indonesian figure fills an alcove in the whitewashed wall of the main entrance hall. The contemporary fresco of a falconer is by Alec Finn, a musician and friend of Sean Ryan. Both belong to an ancient Irish hawking club, and when not playing or restoring, they disappear together over the hills. One corner of the entrance hall has been made more intimate by hanging textiles on the wall and across the draughty doorway. A candelabra casts a warm glow around the room.

LEFT A view through the massive sliding glass doors of the Japanese-inspired tea house takes in the Shanagarry Wetlands, which are used as a staging post by a multitude of different migratory birds.

Potter's Retreat

A casual visitor to Shanagarry may be forgiven for discounting it as a small, anonymous village situated on a flat and relatively uninteresting stretch of the south coast of Ireland, just east of Cork. Yet its name elicits a curious resonance in both bird lovers and collectors of pottery around the world. The Shanagarry Wetlands, overlooking Ballycotton Bay, are one of the most important staging posts in Europe for migratory birds, and the unassuming village is home to new-wave potter Stephen Pearce, whose workshops and factory produce popular lines of earthenware made from clay dug from the Blackwater River.

A man of enormous energy and drive, Stephen Pearce designed and built his house in 1972 for the princely sum of £6,100. It lies a short distance from the pottery which he set up on his own, following a period working with his father, also a potter. At a time when the accepted building technique in this part of Ireland was to set bungalows on stilts, Stephen opted for a more traditional method and dug a large foundation in the ground against the hill which would shelter his house from the wind.

The ground plan of the house which Stephen designed is identical to that of a traditional Irish cottage, with one central room in which pigs and chickens would have gathered, and a fireplace where the cooking was done. Stephen has successfully revisited the old Irish farmhouse design, drawing on traditional ideas while incorporating several

twentieth-century luxuries, such as large windows and underfloor heating.

The Pearce home has come together in stages, each addition to the original plan the result of fundamental changes in Stephen's life. The initial design is based on a simple formula—a symphony of terracotta tiles, natural wood and whitewashed walls. Clutter is banished, each room equipped with deep-set drawers, hidden cupboards and sliding partitions behind which to disguise the detritus produced by his family.

The first major structural change was what he dubbed the 'breeding block', built in 1979 at the far end of the plot and wholly disconnected from the main house. Here Stephen envisaged raising his children, isolating their noise and clutter from his own space, not realizing how impractical this particular vision was to prove. Marriage to his second wife Kim-Mai Mooney and two more children prompted him to rethink, and the block was joined to the house by a series of corridors. Family life now gravitates around the central kitchen, aggrandised in 1993 by a light and airy conservatory, which serves as a spacious dining room. The most recent addition to the property has been dubbed the 'Vietnamese Embassy' and is the wing in which his wife's mother now lives.

A scholarship to Japan in 1965 to study pottery rounded off Stephen's education, yet he returned to Ireland determined not to copy slavishly what he had seen. Decades later, he is ready to admit that the Japanese way of life has subconsciously influenced nearly everything he

LEFT, ABOVE & OPPOSITE A number of art works around the house are by Patrick Scott, Stephen's godfather and mentor, and are composed using gold leaf and a tempera wash. The stark, whitewashed corridor set wth niches and shelves provides a backdrop for displaying shells gathered at the beach and pottery figures.

has achieved: it is reflected in the harmony and design of his home and his current lifestyle as well as in the design of his pottery. An acknowledgment of this lasting influence is the tea-house, tucked away on the water's edge at the end of the gardens. What was initially designed as a small hut where Stephen could take a break from his work to eat a sandwich and

ABOVE LEFT & RIGHT Stephen designed the circular fireplace in the tea house, where he and his wife Kim-Mai meditate. The gold-leaf painting is by Patrick Scott. A modern console table by David Chipperfield which used to display shirts in

the Issey Miyake shop in Sloane Street, London, now graces one wall of the conservatory dining room. A selection of hand-made wooden bowls are the work of Ciaran Forbes, a master wood turner and monk at Glenstall Abbey.

drink a cup of tea has become a building of stature, influenced by a temple in Japan where Emperors would go and sit to watch the moon rise over the lake. Stephen and Kim-Mai go there to meditate, to watch the birds fly in over the water, and to reflect on life.

ABOVE & RIGHT A painting by Mick Mulcahy hangs on one wall of the kitchen above a rustic dresser on which a freshly baked loaf of soda bread is cooling. The small, cosy kitchen links the sitting room and conservatory dining room. Its shelves are filled with Stephen's plates.

ABOVE Stephen has always loved carpentry and the main bedroom is entirely his design. The blueprint for the bed was adapted from a traditional Scandinavian sleigh bed and is made from American ash. The floorboards are Canadian pine.

ABOVE A wall of sliding doors conceals wardrobe space. They are made from canvas on ash-wood frames and are based on Japanese rice paper screens.

A stainless steel chair by Philippe Starck is placed like a piece of sculpture in the entrance hall beneath a painting by Felim Egan. The terracotta tiles conceal underfloor heating, and it is a household custom for shoes to be removed at the front door.

LEFT A limestone plateau, the Burren is today empty and silent. Yet signs of the human past are visible everywhere, from dolmens to forts, ancient fields and churches.

Hidden Worlds

The Burren is probably the most extraordinary landscape in the whole of Ireland. Situated in north Clare, it covers a vast, bare, hilly area devoid of trees and obvious surface water, a barren stretch of mysterious beauty littered with stones, and dissected by indeterminate lines of dry stone walls. Beneath its limestone surface is a labyrinth of caves, streams and underground lakes. Punctuating the skyline at intervals are strange and beautiful monolithic and megalithic tombs, vast flat stones arranged as monuments to an earlier mystical time. Otherwise the plateau seems uncannily empty and silent, as if no contemporary mortal dares set foot amidst the dolmens and forts of its ancient past.

Yet the Burren's deep sense of mysticism holds a strong attraction for those seeking a more

meaningful existence in a world where the pace of life is fast and furious. Within the folds of its terraced mountains and sunken valleys, an amazing variety of houses, cottages and dwellings are tucked away, hidden from the view of passers-by.

Keith Payne is an artist and a traveller who discovered the remains of a small ruin on a patch of land high on the Burren one New Year's Day. Over the ensuing months, Keith restored the property and transformed it into a cosy parlour with a huge fireplace, adding a contemporary two-storey house with a huge studio where he works, relaxes and entertains, and a spiral staircase which leads up to a gallery and bedroom. His paintings and drawings, which are displayed all over the house, are strongly influenced by the dolmens and monoliths visible beyond his window.

While mystical places often inspire people to take up new and alternative lifestyles, it is often in these same areas that the last of the traditional crafts people are found. Gabriel Casey has lived on the Burren all his life and until 1986 was earning his living as a teacher. During a self-imposed sabbatical, he restored a small cottage and worked for a year along the seashore, collecting seaweed and Irish moss.

He is uncertain how he first became involved in making Irish rustic furniture, but remembers the pleasure he experienced cutting his first length of

ABOVE & OPPOSITE Keith Payne's house is framed by the standing stones of the Poulnabrone Dolmen. The compact kitchen of his hideaway is planned around the Rayburn stove, with pots and pans hanging from the ceiling within easy reach.

Goodall's
MIXED HERBS
SAXA
SAXA
SAINSBURY'S
Rosemary
Thyme

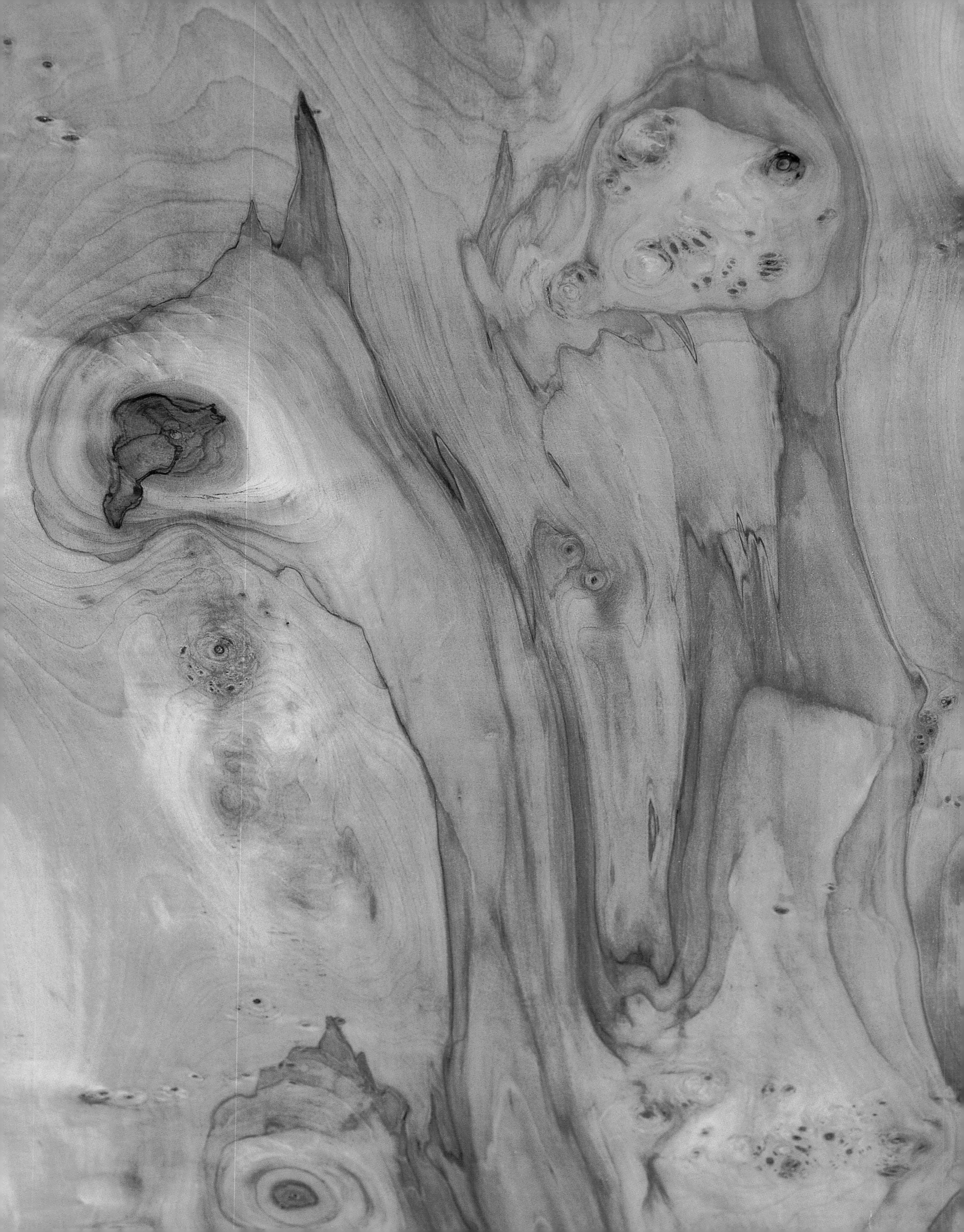

LEFT & OPPOSITE A traditional rocking chair takes shape in Gabriel's workshop: A raw, twisted piece of hawthorn is selected; rockers are fitted to the chair at the end. The texture and grain of wood are an obsession for artisans like Gabriel Casey.

RIGHT Lines of dry stone walls are a familiar sight across the Burren's austere landscape. Keith's living space is divided into his working studio and a sitting area where a comfortable sofa and mismatched armchair crowd a Scandinavian stove. The traditional rocking chair is by Gabriel Casey. The spiral staircase leads up to a bedroom and gallery.

blackthorn to make a chair. From a small, crowded workshop at the back of his cottage, Gabriel gradually taught himself the ancient skills required to make a traditional Irish rocking chair, always considered an important piece of furniture in any Irish house. Today, his rocking chairs and other rustic furniture have established his reputation as far away as America, where his pieces are prized for the simplicity of their design and the rich colour of the wood.

Gabriel cuts the lengths of hawthorn and blackthorn straight from the hedgerows, their tortured forms lending themselves to the natural shape of the rockers. He starts cutting in the dark of November, on a waning moon, and stores the green wood for nearly eighteen months in an old milling parlour until it has dried sufficiently to work on. Each

ABOVE The rustic rope seat of a traditional Irish chair, its rough wooden back and legs bearing the distinctive hallmark of furniture maker Gabriel Casey.

rocking chair is made with the human form in mind—the length of the rockers, the height of the backposts and the depth of the seat of each chair are adapted to fit the individual for whom it is destined.

Gabriel uses traditional tools, working on each chair lovingly; the knots and unique characteristics of each piece of wood are enhanced and burnished with a combination of beeswax and turpentine which bring out the timber's natural colour. The final result resembles more a piece of sculpture than a practical item of furniture and his chairs are instantly recognizable in many homes throughout the Burren.

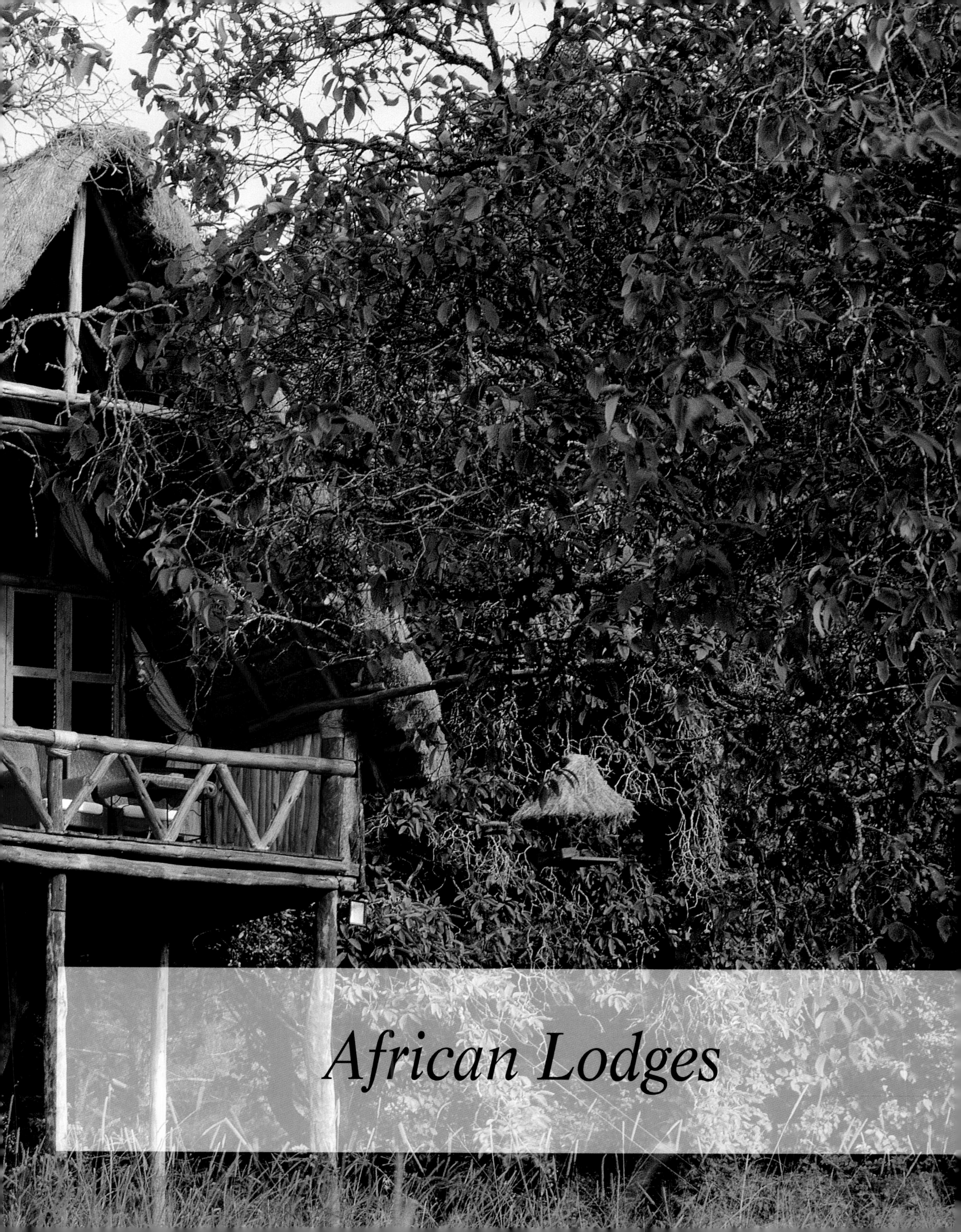

African Lodges

Wilderness Encountered

The dramatic, rocky terrain of Tsavo East National Park does not conform to every visitor's idea of the Kenyan bush. Tsavo is remote and untamed, its wildlife boasting an extraordinary biodiversity. Red elephants, elegant Hirol antelopes, man-eating lions and flocks of vividly colored carmine make the Tsavo their home—and tourism here is tightly controlled in order to preserve the area's unique mix of species.

One of the few safari facilities in Tsavo East, Galdessa Camp makes the national park's wildlife its focus. Camp founder Pierre Mourgue d'Algue works closely with the Kenya Wildlife Service on conservation projects such as the reintroduction of the rare black rhino. It is this close interaction with animals, as well as isolation from human settlement, that gives Galdessa its wild, almost primitive flavour. Guests are accommodated in

LEFT Set by the river in a grove of doum palm trees, the main camp 'mess' provides a communal area for lounging and dining, although meals are also served in more intimate surroundings. In keeping with the philosophy of Galdessa, both the mess building and furnishings are in harmony with the environment. The roof is thatched with grass and the structure's support poles are a replenishable resource—native gums from a plantation. The floor is local Galana stone, and the dining table is made from a stone slab found in the national park.

individual *bandas*. Each of these secluded thatch-roofed tents is built on a timber platform, with walls of mosquito netting and canvas. Elephants, buffalos and rhinos congregate just yards away at the river bed that cuts through the camp.

Inside the *banda*, lamps fashioned from ostrich eggs, gnarled wooden headboards and a bathroom clad in stone enhance the camp's sense of harmony with its surroundings. Creature comforts are equally important though. Each *banda* is powered by solar electricity, with hot water fed through a traditional canvas drum shower in the private bathrooms, and a field telephone links to the kitchen for ordering sundowners or freshly baked croissants. Particular emphasis is placed on the experience of dining in the wild. Evening meals may be enjoyed under the stars, while breakfast is served at camp tables by the river bed as wildlife gathers for a morning drink. Few safari experiences in East Africa are as intense, or as intimate.

RIGHT The viewing platform and sundeck of the Rhino Suite overlook the Galana River and Yatta Escarpment. This secluded vantage point is ideal for observing the rhinos and buffalo that cluster around the river in the early morning and evening, or simply for enjoying a glass of wine and plate of ripe mango.

OPPOSITE & ABOVE The spacious bathrooms include dressing space, closets and a shower room with a stone floor. Each banda *is supplied with running water, but the shower itself is a traditional safari drum, which is filled by hand to the temperature preferred by each guest. Rough bush textures give the bathroom a primitive feel. The stone basin is set into a stack of river rocks, and solar-powered lamps are made from Ostrich eggshells fixed on buffalo vertebrae. In a sunny corner of the room, a seed pod looks startlingly like a snake at first glance.*

Native Elements

From the air, the six neatly thatched cottages and mess buildings comprising Borana Lodge are barely visible. Even approaching them by road, after a long dusty drive from Nairobi, they appear as little more than shadows on the scrubby green hills of the Kenyan highlands. Clinging to a ridge in the Samangua Valley, Borana is the most discreet of safari lodges. Owners Michael and Nicky Dyer and designer Murray Levet shared the same vision for Borana: that it should blend into the surrounding landscape, while providing a stunning viewpoint for observing the area's wealth of wildlife.

The Dyers were captivated by this unspoiled corner of Kenya more than a decade ago, acquiring a 35,000-acre ranch near Timau, north of Mount Kenya, where they farm cattle, sheep and camel. It was only several years ago that they decided to share their patch of wilderness, constructing a lodge compound that would accommodate no more than a dozen paying guests. The result—six thatched huts, two

LEFT Borana blends perfectly with the surrounding countryside, high in the northern frontier district of Kenya.

communal living areas and a dining hall with wide veranda overlooking the valley—are intended to offer a homely and thoroughly relaxing respite from days out on safari.

In keeping with the intentions of Borana, almost every part of the lodge has been made by hand from natural elements. The huts and communal halls are built from fallen cedar trees, collected from the ranch woodlands, and local stone, with pitched roofs thatched with grasses from the swamps. Complementing the rustic structures, the furniture is crafted by artisans from Kenyan rosewood and cedar. The dining chair seats and backs are slung with leather hides from the ranch cattle, and the tradition-

ABOVE The surrounding hills are wooded, but the valley below is fairly dry with whistling thorns, acacia trees, scrub and some open grassland. It is ideal country for game, attracting elephants, greater kudu, water buck, impala, zebra, giraffe and lions.

ally woven wools and cotton textiles used throughout for upholstery, bedcovers and curtains. Against this inviting backdrop, guests are required to do very little: enjoy the hearty meals of game from the ranch and fresh vegetables from the garden; relax on the veranda to watch elephants, lions, zebras and giraffes cluster around the nearby watering hole; or cool down in the natural, rock-edged swimming pool with its superb valley views.

ABOVE & LEFT Like most of the furniture at the lodge, the side table in the living area has been fashioned from a huge, rough-edged slice of fallen cedar. Nestled on top are a clutch of native pottery vessels and a decorated gourd that serves a a lamp base. The private cottages are a showcase for the work of local artists. Fabrics and textiles have been sourced from all over Kenya, and are sewn up on site by an old tailor with an ancient sewing machine. The cottages vary in shape as they have been created to fit into the immediate environment with a minimum of disturbance.

ABOVE & OPPOSITE Decoration of the camp includes one-off details reflecting the natural environment. A painting on the dining room wall depicts the impala that graze on the plains below the lodge. Handles on a cabinet are made from knotted twigs. The roof on the main lodge building and those on the private cottages are made from reed thatch, which is twisted around fine cedar sticks to give an interesting knotted effect from the inside and a typical thatched look from the outside.

Treehouse Hideaway

A few minutes away from the house where Karen Blixen once lived at the foot of her beloved Ngong Hills, a latter-day pioneer has created a most unusual retreat. Unlike the colonial stone cottage of his celebrated former neighbour, Paul Verleysen has constructed a series of treehouses, designed to rise above the long Masai grass and surrounding bushland for unhindered views of the Ngong Hills. His idyllic existence here, running the treehouses as a lodge for safari guests, seems a world away from the pressures of the Belgian diplomatic service, which he left after more than 20 years to pursue an altogether different lifestyle.

Accommodation at Verleysen's lodge, Ngong House, is in one of four treehouses, built on stilts of local olive wood and with grass roofs made in the traditional African way. Each structure is two-storyed, with a terrace, lounge and dining areas and bathroom on the lower level, and a bedroom above. The houses are designed with comfort in mind, yet the interiors have a decidedly rustic feel. Walls and floors are lined in local timber, and furnishings are made from old dhow wood and canoes salvaged from the coast. Verleysen designed and built each of the houses himself, drawing on the talents of regional artists and artisans to add many of the finishing touches,

LEFT Owner Paul Verleysen drew on his background as a construction engineer to build the treehouses himself, an undertaking that took a year and a half. The ten-acre site Verleysen chose for the lodge is a thirty-minute drive from Nairobi, but feels completely isolated with its thick bushland and abundant wildlife.

LEFT In each treehouse, a niche beneath the stairway to the living area is coverted into a cosy sofa for reclining, reading or just admiring the view beyond. Where windows do not offer an outlook, they are filled with beautifully patterned dalle de verre. *One ingenious feature is the entrance hatch, which closes automatically with the help of attached weights.*

such as handwoven rugs, bed-covers and cushion-covers. Even the bathroom sinks are fired in a nearby pottery and painted by a local artist.

At sunset, the outlook from the treehouse terrace is spectacular. From this perch, fifteen feet above the ground, the panorama of the Ngong Hills fades slowly in the evening light, and the sound of lions can be heard close by. It is not hard to imagine Karen Blixen watching a very similar scene from her own veranda half a century earlier.

ABOVE & RIGHT In true safari tradition, evening meals are a special occasion. After drinks around the campfire, guests can enjoy an intimate dinner at their treehouse, where the dining area is centered around a large fireplace. Much of the table setting is produced by Kenyan artists and crafts people. The crockery is fired and glazed locally, while the glassware is made by the same artist responsible for the dalle de verre *windows. Only the silver cutlery and some of the wines are imported.*

ABOVE & OPPOSITE Twenty feet above the ground, the bedrooms provide wonderful views over the tree tops to the Ngong Hills. Each is decorated in a different style—in this treehouse, the look is oriental. The four-poster bed is from Bali and is canopied with yards of fine mosquito netting. The bed cover is from India. With its unfinished wooden walls, the bathrooms in each treehouse appear rough-and-ready, but a closer inspection reveals some luxury touches. The basins with their brass taps are made in local pottery and painted by hand. Also handcrafted are the blue glass bottles and soap containers.

Conditioner

Splendid Isolation

Remoteness was the quality that most appealed to veteran safari guide Richard Bonham when he came across a magnificent corner of northeast Kenya in the Chyulu Hills. The panoramic view over a vast plain to Mt Kilimanjaro, the rich wildlife and the absence of tourism sold him on the location for both his home and lodge. It was the quintessential Africa, with flat-topped acacia tortillas trees and short-grass plains, golden in the dry season and green in the rainy. The downside was that water would have to be hauled 170 miles to serve the site. Undaunted, Bonham undertook a year of negotiations with the Masai elders of the Chyulus to win a concession for 300 acres. The idea was to create a home, but also take in a handful of paying guests.

The focus of home and lodge life is the main 'mess', which serves as both dining and lounge area. Accommodation is in individual thatched cottages, designed with open facades so that guests in bed have uninterrupted views of Mt Kilimanjaro and the savanna below dotted with lions, cheetah, giraffe and zebra. In the absence of a front wall, each of the cottages is raised on stilts to provide security from wild animals that come too close.

As the location is so isolated, Bonham had no choice but to use building materials that could be found nearby. Rocks and boulders were used for construction of the walls. Timber for the main trusses and building frames was collected from the area, but only from fallen trees. The cluster of lodge buildings that comprise Ol Don-yu Wuas—the main mess, five thatched cottages, and Bonham's own house—are designed to be as open as possible. Furnishings are kept simple so that attention is focused on the scenery, fulfilling Richard Bonham's goal that guests feel part of the view rather than simply acting as observers.

LEFT Each of the thatched cottages is designed so that the views can be enjoyed while lying in bed. The cottages look directly out onto a forest of acacia tortillas, with open savanna and the volcanic peak of Mount Kilimanjaro in the distance.

Blake

PREVIOUS SPREAD, ABOVE & OPPOSITE Richard Bonham's living room is an impressive textural mix of natural elements and native art. Both the sofa and dining table were made at the lodge from fallen olive trees, and the upholstery and cushions are in hand-painted fabric from Zimbabwe. The floor is paved with natural stone slabs from Mombasa, and the roof is thatched with coconut palm leaves. The concession supports some 34 species of large mammals, of which elephants form a significant group. A local carving on an interior doorway is a reminder of their presence on the plains below. Due to the lodge's isolated location—minus the usual tourist bustle—encroaching wildlife can be a real threat. Bonham keeps rifles on hand in the event of danger, from top: a 416 Rigby rifle, a 20-gauge Beretta and a 12-gauge Cogswell Harrison.

PREVIOUS SPREAD The furniture in Bonham's own bedroom, like the rest of the lodge, is made from natural materials found on-site. The bed and dressing table are fashioned from a fallen olive tree. Blue mosquito netting, purchased at the fabric bazaar in Nairobi's Biashara Street, adds a shot of electric colour. Blue and white rugs from Guatemala carry through the color theme.

OPPOSITE, LEFT & BELOW Nothing stands between guests and the view they enjoy from their private balcony. Other objects of interest include the straw hats from Mombasa and a silver tea service that belonged to Bonham's grandfather. A tray table stands at the ready for a cooling sundowner, and also provides display space for a native bowl containing mementos of wild Africa.

Tropical Seclusion

ABOVE & OPPOSITE Although the owner lives in Nairobi most of the time, she revels in the solitude and proximity to the beachfront offered by her holiday home. It is only a 200-yard stroll to the waterfront from the colonnaded porch that runs the length of the house.

The coast of Kenya is edged by some of Africa's most beautiful beaches. Rows of towering palm trees, long stretches of white sand and clear, blue-green water are the magnet for weekenders from Nairobi or Mombassa or holidaymakers from abroad. The seaside town of Milindi has already blossomed into a resort, as have other areas along the coast. Those in search of seclusion and unspoilt beaches need to look further afield to find tranquility, like the owner of this house, who guards its location jealously.

With the help of her brother, an engineer, the owner set about building her dream holiday home in 1987 after selling her house in now-bustling Milindi. She used no architect's plans, simply her own sketches and pictures clipped from magazines, which her brother helped to interpret.

LEFT Echoing the fuss-free decorative scheme used throughout the house, the kitchen looks pristine with its white-washed walls and scrubbed wood benches. There is no extraneous detail, and everything in the room has a practical purpose, in line with the owner's belief that a holiday home should be kept free of distractions and be as easy as possible to maintain.

FOLLOWING SPREAD The appeal of this bedroom lies in its monastic simplicity. The carved four-poster bed and printed bedcover provide the only surface decoration. Windows are kept free of drapes as much for effect as ease of maintenance.

RIGHT The traditional thatching of the roof is in a style known as mukuti. *Thick swatches of dried leaves from coconut palms are bound tightly to an intricate timber framework to create a surprisingly waterproof shelter. The furniture on the veranda is made in the traditional style of the coastal region and scattered with cushions in bright prints in a mix of African and Western designs. Here, as elsewhere in the house, the floor is paved in local stone.*

Also crucial to the project was an Indian builder from Mombassa who was skilled in many of the traditional building techniques of Africa's coastal architecture. The house was constructed from blocks of coral, which were then whitewashed, and roofed with a thatch of coconut palm leaves. As there was no electricity in the area, the pace of building was painfully slow, progressing one room at a time.

For the interior, the owner wanted to combine a relaxed mood with local character, in keeping with the beachside lifestyle. Her solution was to look to Kenya's past. In the coastal city of Mombassa she scoured derelict buildings slated for demolition, in search of precious hardwood. She uncovered a wealth of Indian teak, imported to Kenya in early colonial days, as well as furniture, architectural features, even bathroom sinks. This imaginative recycling has enabled the owner to surround herself with an array of beautiful objects and textures, made all the more appealing for their sense of history.

OPPOSITE & ABOVE The open-plan living space features double-height ceilings and a gallery level overlooking the dining area. On the art deco table, bought in Milindi, traditional African digos*—food covers woven from palm leaf—serve both a practical and decorative function.*

Most of the wood used in the interior has been recycled from other sources. The banisters are made from timber reclaimed from demolition sites around Mombassa, while the sofa is fashioned from an antique bedhead carved by the bajuni artisans on the island of Lamu.

Swahili Spirit

Lamu Island is a tiny speck in the Indian Ocean, once a stop on the prosperous trading route of the Arabs. Little seems to have changed in this remote part of Africa since the seventeenth century when it was a hub of Swahili culture. It was this exotic and untouched quality that had drawn Robert and Fiona de Boer to the island for years and eventually persuaded them to buy a majestic home by the beach, Kisimani House. The house was once part of the estates of a wealthy nobleman, the Kalif of Zanzibar, and has been studied by archaeologists, anthropologists and architects for decades, all intrigued by its traditional features and its insight into Swahili culture.

The five-storey mansion is constructed around a sunken central courtyard, with large, open-plan rooms reflecting the commun-al nature of ancient Swahili life. Intricate decorative plaster-

LEFT Stairs lead up through the central courtyard of the house to the terrace on the first floor, where a mass of bougainvillea provides shade and color. Household life tends to focus on this open-air living area, which provides padded banquettes for relaxing, and a dining table and chairs made by Lamu woodworkers.

OPPOSITE & ABOVE In the entry hall, as elsewhere in the house, the ceilings are constructed using durable mangrove poles, which span coral walls up to half a metre thick. Door and window frames are made from bomba kofi, an exotic hardwood. Furnishings are designed in the Swahili style, with the emphasis on comfort and durability. The niches above doorways traditionally provide space for displaying treasure such as porcelain bowls, decorated plates and silverware.

work and carved details give the interior a magical quality, particularly on the ground floor where the harem was once housed. Much work has gone into restoring the interior and exterior features to their former splendour. The existing three-storey house needed replacement of all the structural timbers, restoration of the plasterwork, and installation of electricity and running water. Once the basic elements were in place, designer Rob De Boer evolved plans for another two storeys, which now blend seamlessly with the original.

The De Boers traveled widely in the Islamic world to glean inspiration for their project, and this influence has been carried through to the interior decoration. Typical of Islamic homes, the courtyard is the focus of household life. At Kisimani it has been adapted to use as a dining terrace, with a profusion of greenery providing shade during the day, and an open roof providing impossibly romantic views of the starlit sky at night.

LEFT A bedroom suite recreates the feel of a Swahili harem, with the bed enclosed by curtains of sheer muslin netting. The colourful banas, *or roof joists, are original features, typical of seventeenth-century Swahili architecture on Lamu Island.*

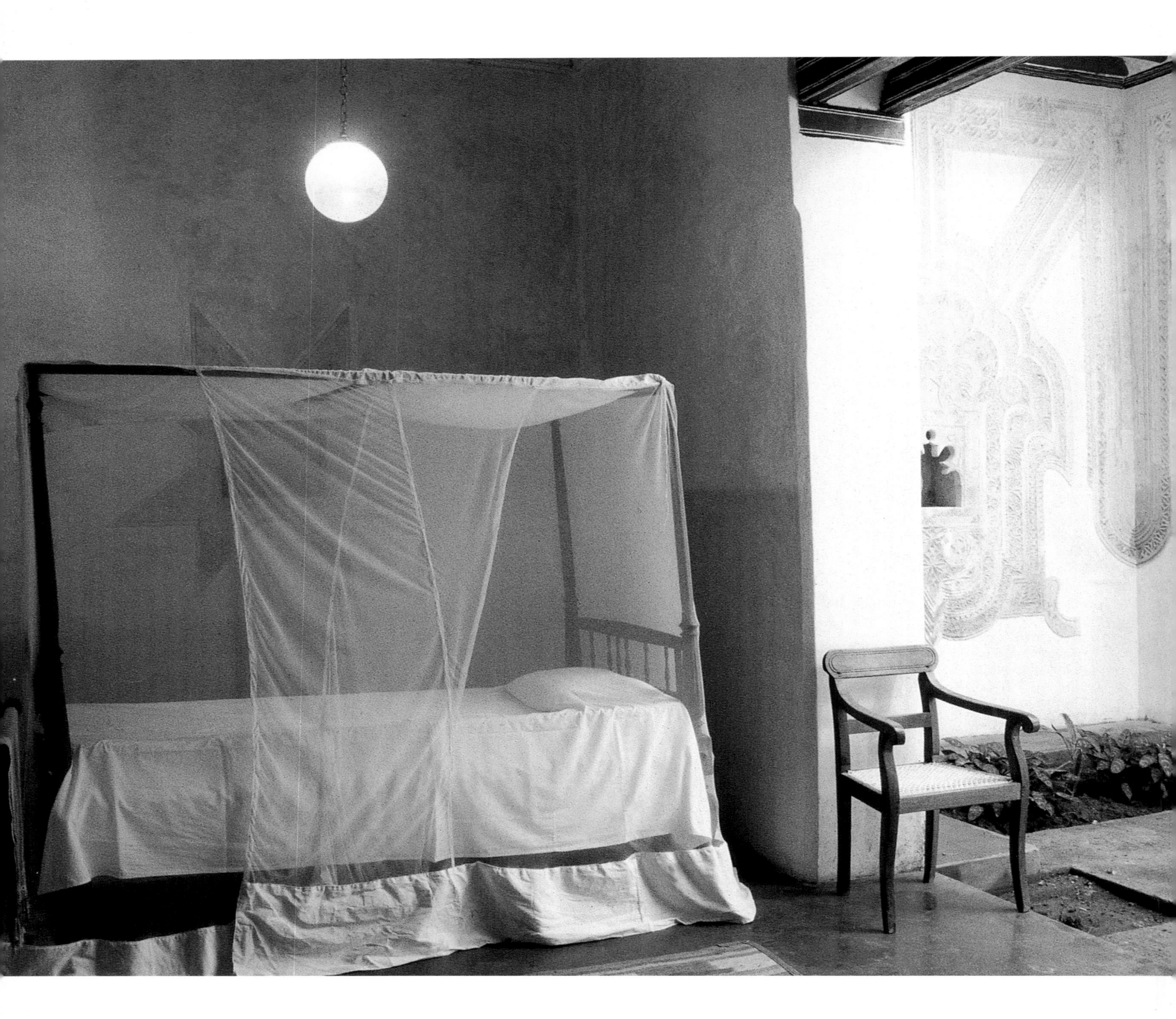

ABOVE & OPPOSITE The ground floor level with its elaborately carved plasterwork once contained the harem. It looks out onto a central courtyard, where a single palm grows up through the house. This area was the setting for important ceremonies such as weddings, traditionally marked by a week of feasting, music and dancing. Adjoining the harem on the ground floor are two seventeenth-century msana, *meaning 'long chamber room' in Swahili. They are marked by elaborate patterns on the plaster-coated walls and niches surrounded by dense carving in the shape of stylized turtles. The chambers now make cool, airy bedrooms.*